The Littlehampton Saga

Osbert Lancaster has delighted many readers with his chronicles of the lives and fortunes of the Littlehampton family of Drayneflete. Here, brought together in one volume for the first time, are the three books in which he celebrates this previously little-known but now celebrated portion of our heritage.

The Saracen's Head is a glorious account of the heroic adventures of a younger member of the Littlehampton family in one of the Crusades; *Drayneflete Revealed* gleefully records the changing fortunes of Drayneflete, its architectural development from village to city and the changing way of life of its inhabitants; and *The Littlehampton Bequest* provides a fully-illustrated catalogue of the magnificent art collection of Drayneflete Abbey which not only reproduces the works of art – from Holbein to Hockney – but also records the achievements and aristocratic personalities of the long line of Littlehamptons.

Osbert Lancaster's delightfully witty but always impeccably scholarly text is complemented by his own delicious drawings.

Methuen Humour Classics

Osbert Lancaster

The Littlehampton Saga

comprising
The Saracen's Head
Drayneflete Revealed
The Littlehampton Bequest

with illustrations by the author

A METHUEN HUMOUR CLASSIC

This paperback volume first published in Great Britain in 1984
by Methuen London Ltd
11 New Fetter Lane, London EC4P 4EE

The Saracen's Head was first published in 1948
Drayneflete Revealed was first published in 1949
The Littlehampton Bequest was first published in 1973
by John Murray (Publishers) Ltd
50 Albemarle Street, London W1X 4BD

Copyright © 1948, 1949, 1973 by Osbert Lancaster

Made and printed in Great Britain
by Richard Clay (The Chaucer Press) Ltd
Bungay, Suffolk

ISBN 0 413 54990 9

Cover illustration: Until very recently the splendid
picture from which this detail is taken, a late work of
Peter Tillemans, hung in the harness-room at
Drayneflete Abbey, where it had become so begrimed
that the figures were no longer readily identifiable.
Indeed, in the old hand-list, it is catalogued as *Queen
Victoria and the Prince Consort at the Aldershot Review.*
When, on the instructions of the present Countess, it
was taken down and carefully cleaned, it was
discovered to be a portrait group of the 1st Earl, his
wife and elder son in the livery of the Drayneflete
Hunt outside the great gates of the Park, of which
each pier bears the proud crest of the Courantsdairs, a
Saracen's Head proper, with, in the background,
Hawksmoor's triumphal column, erected to
commemorate the Glorious Revolution of 1688.

Contents

THE
SARACEN'S HEAD

or
The Reluctant Crusader

FOR CARA AND WILLIAM

Contents

CHAPTER 1

A Call to Arms

NCE upon a time, in the reign of King Richard Coeur-de-Lion to be precise, there lived in Sussex a certain land-owner known as William de Little-hampton. He was exceedingly rich, the lord of five manors with the rights of soccage, corkage and drainage between Chanctonbury Ring and Bognor-supra-Mare and in addition he enjoyed the rare privilege of fishing for sturgeon in the river Arun. (In fact there are no sturgeon in the river Arun but this was nevertheless regarded as a very rare distinction.) His principal residence was the castle of Courantsdair, a large, prominently situated building completely equipped with drawbridge, moat, bailey, keep, posterns, dungeons and all the usual twelfth-century fittings and enjoying a magnificent view of the South Downs and the English Channel. Unfortunately, though immensely strong it had already been built over a hundred years and even by twelfth-century standards was considered more than a little uncomfortable. The fire smoked without stopping, the wind whistled round the great hall through a dozen cracks and none of the window shutters fitted properly, which was all the more noticeable as none of the windows had any glass. William who every year from the beginning of November to the end of May had a constant succession of colds, coughs, bronchitises and influenzas, was fully aware of these defects and had made several attempts to make his home a little more up to date, but he had never yet succeeded in overcoming the resistance of his mother, a remarkably tough old lady of sixty-eight of whom, I am sorry to say, he was very much afraid. Whenever he suggested putting a screen across the entrance to the kitchen or hanging some arras on the walls of his bedroom his mother promptly reminded him that his dear father had never had any such sissy fittings in his day, and what was good enough for old Sir Dagobert should certainly be quite good enough for his son. William invariably agreed, apologised deeply for having raised the matter and tried hard to suppress his sneezes for the rest of the evening in case his mother should think he was playing for sympathy.

Sir Dagobert de Littlehampton, who had died as the result of a most unfortunate accident very shortly after the birth of William, his only son, had been renowned throughout Christendom for his bravery, powers of endurance, exceptional strength and outstanding skill in all manly sports and exercises. At the tender age of two, when lying in his cradle at the windiest corner of the castle battlements (his preferred resting-place), he had been attacked by an enormous but short-sighted hawk which had mistaken the lusty infant for a tender and well-developing pigling. Any other child would undoubtedly have been scared stiff by such a mischance and quite incapable of putting up any resistance. Not so little Dagobert: with his tiny hands he seized the marauder round the throat and by the time his terrified nurse had returned to her charge (she had, I regret to say, been gossiping with a good-looking sentry on duty on the western tower), the intrepid child had wrung the rash bird's neck with every appearance of satisfaction. At the age of six he was taken on his first wild boar hunt and his horse, having the ill-luck to catch his foot in a rabbit-hole, was thrown heavily. Just at that moment the boar, of quite extraordinary size and ferocity, turned round in his tracks and, bellowing horribly, made straight for the prostrate lad. Without a moment's hesitation, and with complete presence of mind, little Dagobert drew out his pocket knife and just as the infuriated beast, which was straddling its prey, was lowering its head to rip the fearless child with its vast tusks, he plunged it into the boar's stomach which with one decisive gesture he slit from end to end. The news of this exploit came to the ears of the King, who chanced to be passing through the neighbourhood at the time. As a token of his admiration, he granted Dagobert the right to bear as his crest a severed boar's head proper, which was why this device was embroidered on the great standard which ever flapped above the keep of Courantsdair. The skull of the animal, complete with tusks and tastefully mounted, hung on the wall of the great hall where it had frequently given William the fright of his life as he came upon it unexpectedly in the dim torch-light on a winter's evening.

By the time Sir Dagobert had reached the age of his son at the opening of our story – twenty years and two months – his fame had spread far and wide. Five times Junior Tilting Champion of the Southern Counties (winning the cup outright in 1138), winner of the All England Archery Competition on two separate occasions and runner-up in the finals of the Mercian Battleaxe Contest in the following year, he had already taken part in two pitched battles, five forays, eleven skirmishes and three sieges. In addition he had killed two knights in single combat ar d unhorsed several more. Of the men-at-arms, archers and common foot soldiers that he had slain he had already long since lost count. But with all these triumphs, which increased as the years passed by, his joy remained incomplete for he had no son and heir. Year after year his wife, a woman of like temper to himself, gave birth to a strapping girl until, at long last, in his sixtieth year his only son was welcomed into the world by eleven sisters. (Six more, less hardy than the others, had died of colds, croop, or bronchitis during the various hard winters.)

Unfortunately Sir Dagobert did not long survive hearing the good news – he never saw little William at all – as just at this time he met his death as the result of the most exceptional ill-luck at the siege of an obscure town near Limoges. It so happened that in the view of the King of England, who was besieging the place, the hour had come to make a final assault and so bring to an end an operation which had already gone on far too long, and, in order to insure the success of this attack, various siege engines of the latest design and enormous power had been brought up. Now Sir Dagobert disapproved on principle of all such new-fangled devices, considering them ungentlemanly, and, in so far as they were not completely useless, likely to discourage a healthy enthusiasm for hand-to-hand fighting and cold steel. The skilled engineers who operated these fearsome and complicated machines he habitually referred to as 'those ruddy plumbers.' Now it so chanced that, on the first morning that a gigantic catapulta had been set up, Sir Dagobert passed by in the company of some other like-minded warriors to whom he was expressing his customary contempt for long-range weapons in general and catapultas in particular, when in order to emphasise his distaste he delivered a

scornful kick with his mailed foot at a small lever projecting from
the framework of the machine. Unfortunately the mechanism was
already wound up and the projection was in fact the lever which
set the whole thing in motion. The next second the gallant old
knight, the pride of Christendom, was hurtling through the air in a
wide arc in the general direction of the besieged town. It was some
minutes after he had made a dramatic landing head first into the
principal square that he realised exactly what had happened and,
when at last the full ridiculousness of his mishap became
apparent, he was so furious that he burst a blood-vessel and died
on the spot. However, as in life so in death, success crowned his
every exploit, for the townspeople were fully convinced that his
unexpected arrival was but the first indication of a large-scale
airborne attack and promptly threw open their gates and sur-
rendered unconditionally.

The King, when he heard the news, gave Sir Dagobert a full military funeral and shipped his body back to England at the taxpayers' expense. The fine old warrior was deeply and sincerely mourned by his disconsolate widow, eleven daughters and

numerous friends and relations, and was buried in the village church beneath a magnificent monument which exists to this day. If you ever chance to visit it pause and reflect for a moment on the virtues and character of the deceased and, bearing in mind his untimely end, remember that it seldom pays to be scornful of Science.

In the years that followed, the Dame de Littlehampton had devoted herself to the upbringing and education of her only son with the fond intent that he should grow to resemble his beloved father as closely as possible and in every way. With this purpose in view she subjected little William from his earliest years to the strictest discipline. The best instructors in such manly pursuits as wrestling, single-stick, boxing, archery and above all tilting were engaged regardless of expense; three times a week in all weathers the little lad was made to follow the boarhounds, staghounds, foxhounds or basset-hounds according to the season; and no matter how cold the day, even in blackest January, he was forced to swim once round the moat before breakfast.

Sad to relate this carefully designed and regularly practised régime had proved a sad failure, for the older William grew the less he resembled his famous parent. Even at a tender age the likeness had never been very marked, for so far was William from overcoming wild boars in his sixth year that he was still mortally afraid of the domestic cat at the age of ten, and the only result of his regular appearance in the hunting-field had been to instil into him just sufficient knowledge and skill to enable him on most occasions to keep as far away from the dangerous quarry as possible.

But of all the fields in which William failed to emulate his father, in none were his shortcomings so noticable as in the tiltyard. In this useful, and, indeed, in his station in life, essential accomplishment, he made no progress whatever. Finding it

sufficiently difficult to retain his seat on a horse at all, he proved quite incapable of aiming his lance at a target at the same time. All was well so long as the horse was proceeding at walking pace – even when it started to trot he retained some control over his weapon – but the moment it broke into a canter all was lost. And so, William de Littlehampton had grown up, despite the careful instruction of innumerable riding-masters, the glorious example of his revered parent, the reproaches and sound wallopings of his disappointed mother and the mockery of his contemporaries, quite unable to keep a Straight Lance.

One fine autumn evening shortly after William had reached his twentieth birthday he was sitting with his mother after dinner in an alcove in the great hall. The Dame had just firmly announced that she had long been wanting a serious talk with her only son and, as they were now quite alone, she proposed to take the opportunity. (The great hall at this hour was completely deserted save for the presence of William's seven unmarried sisters, his cousins Leofric and Gertrude, half a dozen varlets clearing away the dinner, two men-at-arms sharpening battle-axes in a corner, a wandering minstrel tuning his harp, and about a dozen wolfhounds doing nothing in particular.)

'William,' she said, raising her naturally powerful voice in order to be heard above the customary hush, 'you have now reached an age when it is essential that you should without delay accomplish

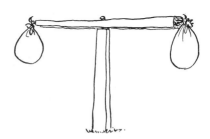

some notable feat of arms in order to gain your position as a knight and bring honour to our house. If indeed,' she added in a nasty tone of voice, 'you have not already passed it. I will not waste time by once more pointing out to you how gravely you have disappointed my fondest hopes, or remarking how thankful I am that your poor father did not live to witness the inglorious career of his only son. I will only say that while we have done our best to conceal from the outside world the graver faults in your character, public opinion now demands that you should vindicate your claim to be the son of the great Sir Dagobert. Moreover, may I point out that even if you are dead to all sense of shame and unmoved by any other decent feelings, you cannot possibly expect to marry your Cousin Gertrude until you have made some small effort to win for yourself a reputation?'

In point of fact William had not the slightest desire to marry his Cousin Gertrude, a bad-tempered girl with a face like a boot, but as both she and his mother had long ago decided that the match was a highly suitable one, he knew better than to attempt to protest.

How long the Dame would have continued to lecture her unfortunate son will never be known, for just as she was about to resume her list of his personal failings, the sound of a long blast upon the horn which hung on a post opposite the drawbridge fell upon their ears. It was a late hour for visitors and instantly there arose within the hall a great bustle and shouting of orders and hurrying to and fro. At last word came from the gatehouse that a solitary monk sought admittance; whereupon the Dame gave order that, provided the sentry was sure that the visitor was really alone, the drawbridge should be lowered.

A few moments later there strode into the hall none other than Abbot Slapjack, a robust and hearty clergyman, who had been the dear friend of the late Sir Dagobert and had long been held in high esteem by the Dame. From his unusual air of self-importance, greater even than his everyday smugness, it was at once obvious that he was the bearer of important news, and as soon as the usual greetings had been exchanged, he took up a commanding position in front of the brazier and, rubbing his hands, launched into an account of his recent travels.

He had, it appeared, been visiting another Monastery of his Order in Canterbury and on his way home to his own Abbey, some

half-dozen miles from the castle, had passed through Rye. There he had noticed alongside the quay a large vessel, which, upon inquiry, he discovered was due to sail in two days' time for the Holy Land.

'As soon as I heard its destination,' he boomed, 'I made all speed to tell you the great news and did not draw rein until I reached your gates. What a chance! How I envy you, dear boy!' he added, slapping William on the back.

Poor William was quite at a loss to know exactly where his good fortune lay or why this information should be thought so exciting. He did not remain long in ignorance. His mother, after barely a second's pause, suddenly clapped her hands and exclaimed with an enthusiasm fully equal to the Abbot's:

'Of course, the Crusade! Why,' she continued, 'we were only discussing this very moment what could be found for William to do. This is exactly the thing. Oh, William, my son, what an opportunity.'

'Aha!' said the Abbot, 'I thought you would be pleased. 'Pon my word, if I were only twenty years younger I'd have gone straight off myself. This young rascal here' – slapping William again harder than ever – 'has all the luck. However, there's no time to lose. The Master has consented to delay his sailing for twenty-four hours, but not a moment longer, so you will all have to set to and start packing right away.'

Poor William's heart sank. He knew very little about the Holy Land or about Crusades, but quite enough to be sure he was quite unsuited to such an enterprise. He would have first to cross the sea, which would certainly make him ill, and then there would be a great deal of hard riding, and it would undoubtedly be more important than ever to keep a straight lance. What little he had heard of the Saracens had been most unfavourable, and there would probably be a lot of snakes, scorpions and possibly dragons. The only thing which gave him any pleasure was the fact that he understood the Holy Land to be very hot and after nineteen winters in Castle Courantsdair he felt he could stand a lot of heat.

However, he did not long have leisure for such gloomy brooding, as the Dame, acting with her usual promptitude on the Abbot's last words, had soon turned the whole castle into a hive of unaccustomed industry.

'Send me the Seneschal, the Head Groom, the Armourer, the Farrier, the Fletcher, and the Wardrobe mistress,' she roared; and as soon as these officials were lined up nervously before her chair she started issuing her orders.

'Seneschal,' she said, 'select at once two trusty men-at-arms to accompany your master on the Crusade, a personal servant and a groom. You, Master of the Horse, pick out the best charger in the stables, two good war-horses and half a dozen pack animals; the Farrier here will see that they are all properly shod and will get ready a sufficient supply of extra horse-shoes to last six months. Armourer, it will be your task carefully to examine your master's chain-mail, patch all holes and clean off any rust. Select and sharpen three swords, six lances and a battle-axe; pick out the best helmet in the armoury and polish it well; and look to the shields, touching up the paint work on the crest where necessary. Having done that, you will get ready complete equipment for two men-at-arms. Meanwhile the Fletcher will prepare six gross of the best arrows, taking care to see that all the heads are properly pointed and that the moth has not got at the feathers.'

Having dismissed the parade the Dame then turned her attention to her daughters giggling with excitement in the corner.

'Now, girls,' she roared, 'stop all that tomfoolery and get out your needles and go at once to the sewing-room. The wardrobe mistress will provide a set of white surcoats on which it will be your proud privilege to sew the red cross of the Crusader. See to it that the stitches are small and you get the crosses on straight.'

'Well, well, that's capital,' said Abbot Slapjack, 'there's only one thing you have forgotten, dear lady.'

'What's that?' asked the Dame.

'Our gallant Crusader here will certainly need a page and I think I know who will want to volunteer.'

'Why of course – little Leofric.'

William groaned inwardly. Although of a kindly nature, if there was one person whom he could not stand at any price it was his Cousin Leofric. This repulsive youth was a noisy, snub-nosed, red-headed, conceited lad some three years younger than himself, for whom his natural dislike had been much increased by the attitude of his family. For from his earliest years Leofric had been good at all the things at which poor William had been noticeably bad, and throughout their youth his excellence had invariably been made a matter of bitter reproach to the latter.

'Look at little Leofric,' the Dame would say, '*he* doesn't cry when he falls off his rocking-horse,' or, 'Leofric is much younger than you are and see how good at single-stick *he* is,' or, 'Leofric doesn't make a fuss about bathing just because there's a little pack ice in the moat.'

Inevitably, as time went on, Leofric made less and less effort to conceal his contempt for his cousin, and nowadays seldom missed an opportunity of humiliating him. Indeed he sometimes went further and played horrid tricks on William, such as slipping a thistle beneath the saddle of his horse, tying up a wild boar in his bedroom, or lending him a joke lance which bent double when he was taking part in a tournament. It was not therefore surprising that the very last person William wanted to accompany him on the Crusade was Leofric. Nevertheless he saw there was no way of preventing it. Leofric himself was delighted with the idea, and the Abbot and his mother were both clearly of the opinion that William ought to consider himself very lucky that so splendid a youth should have consented to go with him as a mere page.

But even worse was to follow.

'I say, Aunt,' said Leofric, 'of course we shall be taking Charlemagne, shan't we?'

Now Charlemagne was a large wolfhound with a fiendish temper, incredibly disobedient and horrible to look at. William, who was not very fond of dogs at any time, simply loathed him: but in vain did he protest that Charlemagne would never stand the heat, or would get stung by a viper, or catch rabies and that it would really be most unkind to take him. All such objections were swept aside by Leofric and it was generally decided that Charlemagne must certainly go too.

It was long past his usual bedtime when William got to his room that night. And even after he had lain down and blown out the rush-light he did not get to sleep. Through the open window came sounds of intense activity in the bailey below, hammers ringing on anvils, grooms shouting to men-at-arms, horses being shod, dogs barking, and drivers and servants running to and fro. Then, just as he was dropping off, in came the Dame to give him a dose, 'Just,' as she said, 'to be on the safe side.' And when finally he did get to sleep it seemed that he had barely closed his eyes before a hearty hammering at the door announced that dawn had broken and he must soon be off.

As soon as the family had finished a light breakfast of pickled pork, brisket of beef, soused herrings, bread, cheese and a hogshead of ale, William was ceremoniously dressed. Leofric, as his page, assisted him into his suit of chainmail, taking good care to pinch him and tweak him as much as he could during the process: his sisters slipped over his head a white surcoat chastely emblazoned with the red cross of a Crusader: and finally his mother girded round his waist Sir Dagobert's favourite sword, the very one the hero had been wearing at the time of his tragic death, accompanying the gesture with a little speech in which she exhorted him always to be worthy of his dear papa and to the honoured name he bore, and ended up by telling him how lucky he should consider himself to be going on so delightful an expedition.

This done, William took leave of his mother, his sisters and his Cousin Gertrude, went out into the courtyard and, Leofric holding his bridle, mounted his grey mare, Lillian. (Luckily, the head groom was an old friend and had thwarted an attempt of Leofric's to substitute for the trustworthy Lillian a spirited charger of his own choosing.) Once safely in the saddle Leofric handed him his lance; Abbot Slapjack, who had insisted on accompanying him to Rye (largely, William suspected, in order to see that he did not contrive to miss the boat), heaved himself onto his horse; the men-at-arms drew up alongside; the sentries all saluted; the gatehouse-keeper flung open the great gates; the gatehouse-keeper's wife burst into tears; the gatehouse-keeper's children yelled and waved; the gatehouse-keeper's dog nearly broke his chain from over-excitement; and, having acknowledged the waves of his mother and his Cousin Gertrude from the battlements by raising his lance (his sisters had all been locked in their rooms by their mother who thought this final scene likely to prove too emotional for their refined temperaments), William rode off across the drawbridge and over the downs, followed by a long string of pack animals and preceded by Charlemagne barking furiously.

CHAPTER 2

A Disagreeable Voyage

 ' ON my word you are in luck,' said Abbot Slap-jack, 'I have never seen a finer ship in my life.'
William, who was standing beside him on the quay at Rye, did not really agree, but knew better than to say so. To him the good ship *St Caradoc* seemed pitifully small, markedly uncomfortable and probably unseaworthy.

The Master was a bluff old sea-dog, smelling strongly of fish, who had already taken a great fancy to Leofric. But he was also rather a snob and took much pleasure in the Littlehampton banner with the severed boar's head proper which was proudly flapping over the stern; this made him very polite to William. Everywhere he went he was accompanied by a one-eyed cockatoo which perched on his shoulder, and the ship's cat. This last was a ferocious-looking animal who would be unlikely, William rightly considered, to get on very well with Charlemagne.

At last the moment of departure arrived. The two men-at-arms, Wolfram and Tungsten, were already aboard: all the luggage had been safely stowed away in the hold; and Lillian was tied up uncomfortably somewhere amidships. All the other horses had had to be sold as there was no room for them on board and would have to be replaced on arrival.

'Well, my boy,' said Abbot Slapjack for the twentieth time, 'how I wish I were in your shoes. Do you know I have still a very good mind to come along too?'

'Oh no, please,' said William hastily, 'whatever would the Abbey do without you?'

'Ah, well, anno domini, anno domini,' replied the Abbot in a self-pitying voice and wiped away a tear on the sleeve of his robe.

'God bless you,' he continued. 'God bless you, dear boy. How I wish—' But he got no further for at that moment Leofric, who had been in a frenzy of impatience to get started, dragged William up the gang-plank. Then, with a great deal of shouting, 'What Ho!' and 'Ahoy there!' and 'Avast ye!' the great sail was hoisted, the anchor was weighed, the rowers thrust out their oars, and they were away.

Over all the grisly details of that terrible voyage we will not linger. It will be sufficient if I tell you that William felt very queer long before the figure of the Abbot waving good-bye on the quay had passed out of sight, and had already been sea-sick twice before they were fairly in mid-channel. Charlemagne and the ship's cat had their first major difference of opinion before the ship had rounded the point and, by the time they were off the mouth of the Arun, William was far too ill even to accompany Leofric, who was feeling fine, up on to the poop to catch a last sight of the towers of Courantsdair just visible on the far ridge of the Downs.

According to the Master it was a quite singularly fortunate voyage, taking only five weeks from Rye to the Pillars of Hercules (as in his old-world way he called the Straits of Gibraltar), but for William it seemed more like five years of continuous tempest. His only comfort lay in the reflection that Charlemagne was enjoying it even less than he was. Whenever the unfortunate hound felt well enough to rampage round the deck he was set on at once by the ship's cat, who was always able to escape when pursued by leaping up the rigging, and whenever he was dropping off into a quiet doze he was immediately woken up by a stream of insults from the cockatoo. Leofric, I need hardly tell you, enjoyed every moment and was for ever climbing up the crow's-nest or taking a hand at the oars.

Once the *St Caradoc* had passed through the Straits and was in the Mediterranean the weather improved; the sun came out; the sea was comparatively calm and William began to feel just a little more cheerful. But not for long.

Hitherto, the principal dangers which threatened them had been from the elements, but now an even more terrible peril arose. These waters were at that time infested by hordes of the most savage and ferocious corsairs and pirates whose appalling and bloodthirsty exploits the Master was never tired of recounting. Every time the look-out man in the crow's-nest called out, 'Sail to Starboard!' (or 'Sail to Port!' as the case might be), all the crew rushed for their bows and arrows, the decks were cleared for action, and William and the two men-at-arms had to put on all their armour and stand-to in the poop. In point of fact, much to Leofric's disappointment, in every case the ship either sheered off over the horizon or turned out, on closer view, to be a friendly

merchantman as terrified of the *St Caradoc* as the *St Caradoc* was of her, but nevertheless the nervous strain proved very trying for William. The more so as Leofric was not above giving a false alarm just to see his cousin fall out of his hammock.

After they had been in the Mediterranean about a week, however, there occurred an incident which did do a little towards cheering up William. As they had not touched at any port since leaving the Bay of Biscay it had become necessary to take on some water, and as all the neighbouring harbours were in the hands of the Infidel they were forced to look out for some barren stretch of coast as far removed as possible from any habitation.

At last one morning the look-out announced that he had seen a likely looking place, a small group of palm trees in the midst of a completely deserted strip of shore, where they might safely land and it seemed probably that fresh water was to be found. Accordingly they drew towards the land with a mariner perched astride the carved bird's head on the prow, dropping a plumb-line at intervals. When at length he decided the ship could safely go no farther everyone took off their breeches, slid down the oars and waded ashore.

Once more to feel the immobile earth beneath the feet was in itself a great pleasure to William, but in addition the long stretch of sandy beach, the palm-trees and the numerous cactuses, which for him were a complete novelty, all combined to make the outing peculiarly delightful. There was, indeed, only one circumstance that in any way tended to mar his pleasure, and that was the behaviour of Charlemagne. Hardly less pleased than his master to find himself on *terra firma* the excitable creature raced madly up and down the beach, poking his nose into every patch of shrub and chasing all the sea-birds in sight, and William correctly foresaw considerable difficulty in persuading his notoriously disobedient hound to return to the ship when the time came.

After all too short a stay, sufficient water was found and taken aboard to last the ship's company until their next port of call. The Master, who was anxious not to remain longer than was necessary in these dangerous parts, gave the signal to return to ship. Obediently William started to retrace his steps, first whistling, then calling, and finally chasing Charlemagne, who had paid no attention at all to the summons. All in vain; the maddening animal no sooner heard his master's voice than he bolted as fast as he could in the opposite direction and poor William, who was always desperately anxious not to make trouble and had fully intended to be among the most prompt in obeying the Master's call, was soon quite miserable with embarrassment and annoyance and had almost reconciled himself to leaving Charlemagne behind (which in fact only his kind-heartedness and understandable fear of what Leofric would say had prevented him doing straightaway), when a terrifying thing happened. Charlemagne, clearly visible, although as far from that section of the beach opposite the ship as he could get, was nosing round a clump of shrubs and cactus and deliberately paying no heed to his master's appeals. Suddenly there was a terrible roar, the bushes parted and there leapt out an enormous Numidian lion! Charlemagne gave one terrified

squeak, leapt about six foot in the air, turning round as he did so (no easy feat), and bolted towards the ship as fast as he could. But not fast enough. The lion's first leap landed just short of the wretched animal himself, but not on his tail, which with one snap of its powerful jaws it severed at the roots.

At the first roar William, together with all those of the crew who still remained ashore, had made all haste they could to regain the ship and had the lion not stopped first to taste and then, almost immediately to spit out his tail, Charlemagne's chances of survival would have been slim indeed. As it was, this momentary pause gave him just sufficient start and he was able, in one final bound, to leap from the water's edge onto the gunwale of the ship, leaving the Numidian lion gnashing his teeth on the sands below.

Although Charlemagne's beauty, such as it was, was for ever spoiled, the adventure had not been without advantage to his character. From now on he came racing to heel at the first whistle and if ever he showed any signs of lingering or in any way getting out of hand, William had only to say in a meaning tone of voice, 'There's a good dog, and would he wag his tail then!' to reduce him at once to a state of unquestioning and shamefaced obedience.

The rest of the voyage was relatively uneventful. The sea continued calm; they soon passed out of the waters where corsairs were particularly to be feared, and Charlemagne no longer had the heart to quarrel with the ship's cat and even learned to bear with exemplary patience the appalling behaviour of the cockatoo who made a practice, whenever he appeared, of imitating a lion's roar and calling out such remarks as 'Where's your tail, cocky?' or 'Any old lion, any old lion?'

In due course they came in sight of Cyprus, where they understood the King of England, together with his army, to be still encamped, and William's gloom at the prospect of meeting his comrades-in-arms returned in full force. However, on arrival they discovered that the English contingent had left some days earlier and was already in the Holy Land. William, although careful to express a lively disappointment in conversation with the Master and Leofric, was so much relieved that he was able quite to enjoy the two days they spent in port, which he employed in viewing the principal sights of Limmasol and buying some suitable mementos to take back to his mother, Gertrude and his eleven sisters. However, this respite was but short and the *St Caradoc* was soon once more at sea.

One morning, five days later, William was awakened by the joyful cry of Leofric, who in his enthusiasm had spent almost the whole time after leaving Cyprus aloft in the crow's-nest, announc-

ing that at long last they were in sight of the Holy Land.

As they drew near the shore they could clearly distinguish a large encampment which, judging from the sounds of dogs barking, snatches of tuneless song, and hearty but rather coarse jokes, which floated across the water, they rightly concluded to shelter the English Army. In order that there might be no mistake, however, it was decided that Leofric should go ashore to make enquiries while William superintended the collection of the baggage on deck.

After about half an hour Leofric returned in high spirits. It was indeed the English Army, or a part of it, and they were most fortunate in the time of their arrival for to-morrow at dawn the whole force were to strike camp and march down the coast to join the main body which, under the command of the King himself, had gone ahead to lay siege to Acre. Leofric had already, so he joyfully declared, met many old friends and there was now nothing to prevent them going ashore right away. William, who knew some of Leofric's old friends, tried to conceal his alarm and look properly pleased, and having taken a touching farewell of the Master (unnecessarily touching, William thought, remembering the high price they had had to pay for their fare), the whole party waded ashore and set out at once for the camp.

On arrival at the guard-house, Leofric, who appeared to have acquired quite an extraordinary amount of information in the short time he had spent ashore, gave the password and led William at once to the tent of the commanding officer. The Baron of Barking-West was a formidable old warrior with a complexion which was nearer puce than crimson and very prominent light blue eyes. He had been, it seemed, a companion-in-arms of the late Sir Dagobert de Littlehampton and extended what appeared to be a cordial welcome to his son. Nevertheless William felt that only good breeding prevented him giving expression to a pained incredulity that his old friend could ever have sired so poor a fish as stood before him at this moment. Having been told that he was to be on parade at dawn to-morrow, at which hour the whole force was moving off on their three-day march to join the King, William was dismissed by the Baron, who instructed an orderly to conduct him to the mess.

When William entered the large tent which served as the Knights' mess, dinner was shortly to begin although as yet not all the company were at the table. In particular two knights were still standing up at the end farthest removed from the door as though awaiting his arrival. These William was horrified to recognise as two old acquaintances.

Sir Simon de Gatwick ('Gatters,' to his numerous friends) and Sir Willibald de Wandsworth had been known to William since childhood through innumerable, and usually painful, encounters in the hunting field and at tournaments. The first was a celebrated and highly popular sportsman of fine physique and proven courage. The second, hardly less esteemed, was celebrated for miles round his large estates on the North Downs for his ready wit, unconquerable cheerfulness and extraordinary talent for elaborate practical jokes. William, while admiring the energy of the one and the humour of the other, felt nothing approaching friendship for either and heartily wished that fortune had not thrown them together. Moreover, ever doubtful that his undistinguished appearance would prove familiar even to close friends, he was in two minds as to whether or not so popular and celebrated a pair would even remember him.

He need not have worried. No sooner was he fairly inside the tent when a roar of welcome greeted him.

'Well, well, look who's here!' bawled Sir Simon.

''Pon my soul if it isn't little Willy Littlehampton,' echoed Sir Willibald.

'Whoever would have thought of seeing *him* here,' in chorus.

Smiling nervously William advanced with hand politely outstretched, but unfortunately when he was half-way across the tent, all too conscious that all eyes were upon him, he was so unlucky as to trip over his sword (or rather Sir Dagobert's, and three sizes too large) and fall flat on his face. After a second's ghastly silence a great shout of laughter went up on all sides and poor William, blushing crimson, was picked up by Sir Willibald and brushed down just in time to take his place at table before the entry of the Baron.

But, alas, his humiliations were not yet at an end. Whether through nervousness, or due to the hearty slaps on the back with which he had been welcomed by Sir Simon, before ever he had had a mouthful to eat or drink, William developed the most fearful hiccups. In vain did he try to conceal his plight and avoid all conversation. The Baron, considering it his duty to make the son of his old friend feel at home on his first night, insisted on asking him a string of what he hoped were reassuring questions. How was his dear mother? Did he leave all his pretty sisters in good health? What sort of harvest had they had in Sussex this year? To all these William did his best to reply.

'Very well – hic – thank you. It was been a – hic – good year for oats, but – hic – the barley has – hic hic – been too long in – hic – the ear. Ooop.'

His plight was now obvious to all and a wave of titters went round the tent. Sir Willibald de Wandsworth, however, in contrast to the rest of the company, seemed genuinely concerned, and insisted that the only cure was to drink a mugful of water straight down while holding the nose. He ordered his own page to fetch a mug and, when it was brought, most kindly held William's nose for him while he drank insisting that there must be no heel-taps. Gratefully William threw back his head and swallowed hard. The next moment he thought his end had come. His eyes bulged from their sockets; his mouth, throat and stomach seemed all suddenly to have burst into flame, and he was spluttering and gasping for breath like a drowning man. When at last he regained sufficient composure to notice what was happening around him, the whole of the company, including even the Baron, was in fits of laughter, and Sir Willibald, who had filled the mug not with water but a colourless local drink called Arak, of incredible potency and fierceness, was being congratulated on all sides.

To what further indignities William might have been subjected, had not the Baron intervened, we shall never know. But in fact for the rest of the meal he was left in peace, and so exhausted was he that not even an apple-pie bed which, he discovered on returning to his tent, had been made for him, nor even the couple of desert foxes which someone thoughtfully let loose under his tent-flap round about midnight, prevented him from at once sinking into a profound sleep.

Next morning, long before it was light William, together with the rest of the camp, was aroused by a prolonged blowing of bugles and after a short but busy interval of dressing, packing and parading, he found himself, just as dawn was breaking, one of a long line of horsemen jogging southward across the rosy desert.

CHAPTER 3

Incompetence Justified

HEN the cavalcade of knights and men-at-arms had been riding for about three hours they came to a point where the desert track divided; one branch swung away to the right; the other continued straight on towards some low hills on the horizon. While the Baron was still consulting with his lieutenants as to which route to take there appeared a pair of pilgrims of a very holy but sadly scruffy appearance. Upon being questioned these venerable men assured the Baron that both tracks would lead them to the city of Acre, but advised strongly that they should take the one to the right although, when pressed, they readily admitted it was considerably longer.

'Why, O holy men,' asked the Baron, 'do you recommend us, who you must know to be anxious to rejoin our sovereign with all possible speed, to take the longer way?'

[41]

'O Lord,' replied the elder, holier and dirtier of the pair, 'were you to continue on the road ahead your path would lie directly beneath the walls of the castle of the fearful Almanazor-el-Babooni, whose ferocity, strength and insatiable appetite for Christian blood have made his name a by-word throughout the East. No one has ever yet crossed that pass without his leave and come down on the other side alive.'

'O miserable, snivelling rogues; do you dare to suggest that fear of one contemptible Hottentot is likely to deter a company such as ours: that a force that includes such renowned warriors as the lord of Potters Bar, Tooting Bec, Bromley Common and East Grinstead, as well as innumerable knights of the highest reputation, can be diverted from their chosen route by old wives' tales such as these? Do you dare to suppose that any man of us could ever again show his face in Earl's Court, or even Baron's Court, if we were to give a moment's heed to your craven warnings?'

'Hi there,' the Baron, by now deep purple with rage, called to some men-at-arms, 'seize these insolent scarecrows, and teach them the respect due to their betters.'

Whereupon two lusty fellows rushed at the unfortunate holy men, belabouring them soundly with the flats of their swords, and continued this treatment until at last their victims ran bawling away down the hill. By the time they had rejoined their companions the little force was already some distance along the road which led to the mountains.

From now on until they reached the top of the pass the greatest excitement prevailed among the crusaders. It was generally agreed that the Baron had acted most properly in his summary rejection of the pilgrims' advice and the only doubt which was expressed was as to whether he had not been over-lenient in his treatment of the wretches and whether it might not have been better to have strung them up by the roadside with a short notice pinned round their necks recounting their crime by way of warning to others who went about spreading alarm and despondency in this way.

The only person who did not fully share in the general confidence, you will not perhaps be surprised to hear, was William de Littlehampton. To him it seemed just possible that the Holy Men, who had obviously been a long time in this part of the world, might know what they were talking about. In particular he felt that his companions might possibly be underrating the Infidel tyrant whom, for his part, he was quite willing to believe every bit as formidable as he sounded. However, he knew enough to keep these unworthy doubts to himself.

Suddenly, less than an hour after the meeting with the pilgrims, a loud cry from the advance guard, who had reached the point where the road began to descend to the plain, brought the whole cavalcade to a halt. When William, who crowded forward with the others, reached the spot whence the cry had come, he saw immediately below a level stretch of country dominated by the walls and towers of a powerful castle in the Saracen style. Immediately in front of its gates there was already drawn up what appeared to him to be an enormous host, their spears and scimitars flashing in the bright sunlight.

While the Baron and the more experienced knights who had reined in their horses at the foot of the hill were still discussing the best plan of campaign, a solitary horseman was observed to detach himself from the enemy ranks and come spurring across the intervening desert in a cloud of dust. When he had come within a hundred paces of the knights he pulled in his horse in a most dramatic manner, causing it to rear back on its haunches, and as soon as the dust had subsided was clearly seen to be a coal-black negro of gigantic size, grasping a huge banner richly embroidered with incomprehensible hieroglyphics. Before the crusaders had fully recovered from their surprise the blackamoor herald, for such he proved to be, called out in an enormous voice and quite passable French that he was the servant of the illustrious, all-powerful, and most pious lord Alamanazor-el-Babooni on whose territory they were now standing and who would suffer no Christian pig to remain alive for more than five minutes. So let them instantly begone! If, however, they were so foolish to persist in their purpose his unconquerable master would be delighted to meet as many knights as would care to come against him in single combat.

This challenge, I need hardly say, was at once accepted and while the herald was returning to his own lines to report, an eager dispute was carried on among all the knights as to who should have the honour of dispatching this Infidel braggart. At length, further discussion was prevented by the Baron of Barking-West deciding that, dearly as he would himself have loved to teach the Infidels a good lesson he felt that it would only be fair to the younger knights, who probably had hitherto had few opportunities to prove their worth, if one of them were selected for the task. He accordingly commanded that the challenge should be taken up by Sir Simon de Gatwick, than whom no one of his generation enjoyed a higher reputation. Instantly there was a flood of congratulations for Sir Simon, together with hearty slaps on the back and cries of 'Good Old Gatters,' 'Some people have all the luck,' 'You beat the daylight out of him, old man,' and such like, which was only brought to a close by the sight of the herald returning accompanied by another horseman who could only be the terrible Almanazor himself.

William, as soon as the pair had come clearly into view, felt that his worst fears had been well founded. El Babooni was a man of powerful physique with a great forked beard through which his sharp teeth gleamed like marble tombstones in an overgrown graveyard. On his head was a spiked golden helmet round which was bound a striped turban; in his left hand he held a small round shield, while with his right he whirled an enormous scimitar with what William felt to be a deceptive nonchalance.

However, his companions seemed in no way to share William's

nervous fears. They remarked slightingly on the size of the champion's steed, which indeed, compared with their own great cart-horses, looked small enough; they likened his shield to a saucepan lid; and his general appearance struck them as theatrical and flashy. It was generally felt, and by no one more strongly than that warrior himself, that Sir Simon would have a walk-over.

At length the last encouragements had been given and the saddle-girth finally adjusted and Sir Simon, having put on his great helm, taken his lance from his page and saluted the Baron, urged his horse forward towards the spot where the Infidel champion was impatiently awaiting him.

As Sir Simon, his shield held firmly across his body, his lance as straight and inflexible as a shaft of light, approached nearer his victim, his horse broke first into a trot, then into a canter and finally into a full gallop. El Babooni for his part never moved, and as his opponent came closer and closer all the spectators held their breath, wondering if he were mad. Then, just as it appeared that nothing could now prevent the point of Sir Simon's lance transfixing the insolent Paynim, El Babooni's little black horse seemed to shy abruptly to the right, his little round shield shot out to catch and deflect the menacing spearhead and, as Sir Simon careered harmlessly by, with a seemingly careless sweep of his scimitar he severed the unfortunate knight's head neatly from his shoulders.

At first the Crusaders were too astonished to speak, but when the initial shock had subsided there broke out a flood of explanations and regrets: 'Poor old Gatters.' 'Dashed bad luck.' 'Why, if that wretched little pony hadn't shied at the last moment that nigger would have been skewered as sure as eggs is eggs.'

Almost at once the question arose as to who was to have the honour of taking the place of poor Sir Simon and of avenging his death, but it was soon obvious that this honour belonged by right to his dearest friend, Sir Willibald de Wandsworth.

Once more after the last encouragements had been given and the saddle-girth finally adjusted, a Christian knight, having put on his great helm, taken his lance from his page and saluted the Baron, urged his horse towards the spot where the Infidel champion was impatiently awaiting him.

As Sir Willibald, his shield held firmly across his body, his lance as straight and inflexible as a shaft of light, approached nearer his victim, his horse broke first into a trot, then into a canter and

finally into a full gallop. El Babooni for his part never moved, and as his opponent came closer and closer all the spectators held their breath, wondering, though this time rather less hopefully, if he were mad. Then, just as it appeared that nothing could now prevent the point of Sir Willibald's lance transfixing the insolent Paynim, El Babooni's little black horse seemed to shy abruptly to the left, his little round shield shot out to catch and deflect the menacing spearhead and, as Sir Willibald careered harmlessly by, with an undoubtedly disdainful sweep of his mailed fist, not troubling to raise the scimitar which hung idle at his saddlebow, he caught the unfortunate knight a light clip under the jaw, lifting him clean out of the saddle and breaking his neck with the sound of a whip-crack.

This time the Crusaders were silent for much longer and when finally they had got over their astonishment, although their regrets were as sincerely expressed as before, their explanations were offered with rather a less confident ring. Moreover, the question of who next should take his place in the lists was not so easily to be decided, and had the Baron not firmly intervened the dispute might have gone on for some time.

'Men,' he said, 'I know that each one of you is burning with unquenchable eagerness to press forward and avenge your unfortunate companions. As there is now none among you who can justly be said to excel all others in martial virtues, I have decided that it would be fairest to all to draw lots. Thus you will all stand an equal chance of fulfilling the task which I know is closest to your hearts.'

Having thus spoken the Baron called to the Chaplain and borrowing from him a small piece of parchment carefully divided it with his knife into small slips equal in number to the knights present. These were then handed round by a page and, after each knight had written down his name (or, in rather a large number of cases, made his mark), were collected and placed in a helmet. The Baron, as soon as the helmet had been well shaken, closed his eyes tightly, put his hand and drew forth a slip of parchment. With what keen, if suppressed excitement, did the company wait as the Baron fumblingly, for he had forgotten to remove his mailed gloves, unfolded the selected slip! How tensely did all hold their breath as they observed a look of surprise and then of humorous resignation pass across his face as he scanned the name! How completely they all failed to suppress a gasp, whether of astonishment or relief it would be hard to say, as at last in clear ringing tones he announced the name, 'William de Littlehampton!'

At first poor William could hardly believe his ears and then, as the full truth dawned on him, his head seemed to revolve rapidly on his shoulders and his stomach to start turning over inside him very, very slowly. When at length he had gained some little control over himself, he became aware of a chorus of hearty congratulations on his luck, in which, hazy as he was, he still thought he was able to distinguish a faint note of insincerity. Before, however, he could pause to consider this point his lance was being thrust into his hand by Leofric, his helm set firmly on his head by willing but unknown hands, and poor Lillian, who was hardly less nervous than he, was being urged forward to the point from which Sir Simon and Sir Willibald had started their ill-fated charges. As, obediently and seemingly without his direction, Lillian broke first into a trot, then into a canter, and finally into a gallop, William, thankful at least that his pale green face was hidden by his helm, repeated hopelessly to himself, 'Keep a straight lance, keep a straight lance, at all costs keep a straight lance.' Alas, even as he repeated those words he felt the point of his lance starting to move slowly from side to side and then up and down until it was behaving exactly like a weathercock on a gusty day. 'It's no good,' he thought, 'my end has come. If *only* I had tried harder and paid more attention to all those lessons in the tiltyard. But it's all too late!'

He was now within a few yards of El Babooni and, as he looked at the ferocious countenance drawing rapidly closer, the sight struck him as so appalling that he firmly resolved to close his eyes, never expecting to open them again in this world.

The next thing William knew, there was a crash so terrible that he was sure every bone in his body was shattered, and he felt himself flying through the air and bumped down with a force which set twinkling before his eyes a million stars which were almost at once extinguished by a wave of impenetrable blackness.

After what seemed to him to be several centuries William found himself sitting on the ground struggling to remove his helm which had apparently got twisted round in his fall. When he finally succeeded in getting it off, with what incredulous astonishment did he survey the scene that presented itself to his gaze! A dozen yards away lay the prostrate form of Almanazor-el-Babooni with the broken shaft of William's lance sticking up from the centre of his chest like a skewer in a partridge. Away in the distance a black horse was cantering terrified towards the horizon while, close at hand, Lillian was happily browsing on some cactus bushes. From the ranks of the Crusaders there rose a sound of prolonged cheering, while the negro herald was down on his knees swaying from side to side and wailing like a banshee.

After a few moments, for his wits were still a little bemused by his fall, he began to realise, that unlikely as it seemed, he must himself have been responsible in some mysterious way for the overthrow of El Babooni. Exactly how it had come about he was at a complete loss to explain.

What in fact had happened was this. Almanazor-el-Babooni had hitherto only been accustomed to giving battle to the most accomplished and highly trained Christian knights, such as Sir Simon and Sir Willibald, who invariably charged with a perfectly straight lance. When, therefore, he saw approaching a horseman whose lance, so far from being inflexibly straight, wavered from side to side, describing circles with its point, he was completely dumbfounded and his carefully acquired technique became of no avail. First he thrust out his little shield to the left, then to the right, and finally, too late, straight in front, muffed it and only succeeded in deflecting the point of Sir William's lance into the exact centre of his own chest. Which all goes to show that it is seldom wise implicity to trust the experts.

As soon as they saw the downfall of El Babooni and realised that he would never rise again all the Crusaders came crowding round the still dazed William, slapping him on the back, and wringing his hand. The Baron with tears in his eyes constantly repeated how much he wished his dear old friend Sir Dagobert had survived to witness the events to-day, and repeatedly remarked what joy the news would give at Courantsdair. Natural and proper as were the reactions of William's companions, the extraordinary perform-ance of one bystander was completely unexpected. Much to the general surprise there came thrusting his way through the crowd of knights the gigantic negro herald, whose name strangely enough turned out to be Hercule, who, flinging himself full length on the ground, seized William's right foot and placed it on his own head, informing the company as he did so that he now considered himself the slave of the conqueror of El Babooni for life, and vowing that from henceforth he would never leave his side.

This touching scene might well have continued for some time

had not the Baron called attention to the fact that although Almanazor himself had been dealt with, there still remained his army and his fortress. Accordingly he gave the order to mount and the whole body of knights, with the addition of Hercule, continued in line across the desert towards the enemy.

Any anxiety which the Crusaders may have felt at being faced with what was still a considerable force was soon dispelled by the behaviour of the Infidel host, who ever since they had realised that their leader was laid permanently low had been howling and yelling fit to burst. Now on seeing the approaching line of horsemen they broke and scattered in all directions, some galloping away towards the mountains as fast as they could and some flying back to the fortress, while others followed the example of Hercule and came rushing forward to throw their arms at the conqueror's feet.

On arriving at the great gates of the stronghold the Christians were surprised to find them open, and no single warrior prepared to make any resistance. Accordingly the Baron, having taken suitable precautions against ambush, and secured a number of hostages whom he caused Hercule to announce in Arabic would be immediately beheaded at the first sign of treachery, the whole force entered the city. Their first action was immediately to requisition the largest available palace, naturally El Babooni's, and as much food and drink as they could lay hands on. This done the Baron, having posted a full quota of sentries, dismissed the parade, announcing that all would assemble in the great court of the palace at seven o'clock sharp, when a magnificent banquet would be held to celebrate the happy events of the day.

That evening proved to be one of the most memorable in William's life. Having lived for the past two months on ship's biscuits and salt pork, he had looked forward eagerly to the banquet, but little dreamt how rich and varied the dishes would prove. There were lobsters cooked in wine, red mullets fried in butter, lark pies, fricassee of nightingales' tongues, the tenderest kidneys wrapped in vine leaves and eaten on spits, young gazelles' trotters stewed in honey, mangoes, grapes, little figs, cakes made with almonds, and any amount of wine of all colours cooled with snow. But perhaps the most splendid dish of all was a roast flamingo stuffed with a whole turkey, which was stuffed with a whole goose, which was stuffed with a whole duck, which was stuffed with a whole chicken, which was stuffed with a whole partridge, which was stuffed with a whole quail, which was stuffed with a whole snipe, which was stuffed with a whole lark, which was stuffed with a whole nightingale, which was stuffed with a locust. None of the Crusaders had ever eaten such a meal before; but for William whose mother had never approved of fancy, 'frenchified' dishes and had always insisted at Courantsdair on what she called 'good plain English cooking,' it was a revelation.

After they had all eaten so much they could no longer move, there took place a series of splendid and varied entertainments. There were dancers who whirled round so fast that their limbs seemed about to fly off; there were acrobats who balanced on the

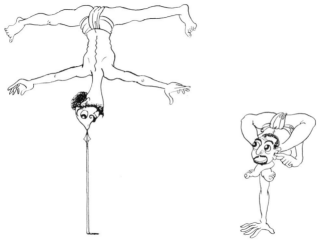

tips of their noses on spears; there were contortionists who tied their legs in knots behind their ears; there were jugglers who kept a dozen oranges, sixteen plates, any number of knives and a quantity of flaming torches all whirling through the air at the same time.

But at last the Baron rose up and announced that as an early start would have to be made in the morning, all should now go to bed.

'However,' he concluded, 'before you depart there is one more toast which I would like to propose. Gentlemen, I give you the health of William de Littlehampton!'

CHAPTER 4

Virtue Rewarded

HE next day was very hot, and as the sun mounted higher in the sky, the Crusaders grew redder and damper, and many complaints arose, especially from the fatter knights, about having to wear armour. But the Baron was very firm and refused for a moment to consider withdrawing his orders. 'You are all on active service now, not just going to a tournament,' he said. 'Besides,' he added, 'this is not really hot – you should have been on the second Crusade. Now that really *was* hot! I remember once in the desert the sun was so powerful that I fried an egg on my helmet. The trouble is you young fellows don't know what real heat is.'

William, who had passed his whole life at Courantsdair, was in no position to contradict and, anyhow, being quite thin he was not suffering unduly. Poor Lillian, however, was in a dreadful state and felt very envious of those horses that were wearing long linen surcoats, tastefully embroidered with their master's arms. William, therefore, determined to have one of these coats, which he much admired, as soon as they reached the camp. Hitherto he had felt that were he at once to adopt this fashion, which he noted was confined to the smarter and more experienced knights, he might be considered to be rather bumptious and guilty of a desire to show off, since the events of yesterday he felt his position among his companions was now sufficiently well established to enable him to do so without arousing any adverse comment.

Shortly after midday the leading knights saw, away in the distance between a gap in the low hills, a patch of brilliantly blue sea and within an hour they were in view of the towers and walls of Acre with the innumerable tents that sheltered the allied armies drawn up in a vast half circle in the foreground.

As soon as they had passed the first outposts the scene was one of the utmost liveliness and bustle, and William would indeed have been hopelessly confused and at a loss to understand the significance of half that met his eyes had it not been for the companionship of Sir Cuthbert de Brett who was riding alongside him. This amiable and well-informed young knight was counted the best amateur herald of his generation, and proved a mine of interesting and detailed information.

'Why look, dear boy,' he said, pointing to a large banner flapping above a tent on the left, 'there are the three rognons braisés on a ground argent of Salamandre de Vichy-Celestins. He, you know, is one of the richest lords in France and owns the best fishing in all Aquitaine. And next door I see the impaled turbot proper of Bobo Sissinghurst, one of the Derbyshire Sissinghursts and uncle by marriage of poor Gatters. And, there, I do believe are the quartered pelicans of Alfredo Frangipani; he, you realise, is Duke of Acqua-Pellegrino and possesses immense estates in Calabria and is directly descended from Romulus' wolf. Oddly enough,' he added in a casual voice, 'he is a connection of mine on his mother's side.'

William, who had never been very good at heraldry, was profoundly grateful for all this valuable information, although the thought of the distinction and grandeur of so many of these names made him feel increasingly nervous. Sir Cuthbert, on the other hand, seemed to find the atmosphere positively exhilarating and kept on repeating in tones of the greatest satisfaction and surprise, 'My *dear*, the whole *world* seems to be here.'

The Baron of Barking-West, after many enquiries from friends and acquaintances, at last succeeded in finding the billeting officer, and, after a considerable delay during which this worthy fellow read through a long list three times, then decided it was the wrong one, sent for another and finally found what he wanted in the first, they were at last, just as the sun was setting, directed to the quarters they were to occupy for the night.

Quite early next morning, before indeed William had finished dressing, he was surprised to receive a visit from the Baron carrying a large parcel done up in a damp cloth.

'Well,' said his visitor with some satisfaction, 'I've fixed it. His Majesty, whom news of your remarkable exploit had already reached, has graciously expressed his wish to make your acquaintance and I am to present you to him at this morning's levée which is due to take place in half an hour.'

At first William was too overcome to reply, and busied himself with finishing his toilet and asking Leofric to give his helmet an extra polish and put on a clean surcoat. When at last he had got over his surprise, he hastily enquired what he was expected to do, how he should address his sovereign and, particularly, what was in the large parcel.

'Ah, yes, indeed,' said the Baron, 'that's a small present for you to give His Majesty. It is always as well on these occasions to have some trifling little memento to offer. And this, I flatter myself, will be much appreciated.' Whereupon, winking broadly, he whisked off the cloth revealing to the horrified William the severed head of Almanazor-el-Babooni!

'Yes,' continued the Baron, 'I had it cut off yesterday with just this purpose in mind. I think you'll find that it will give much pleasure to the Monarch.'

William, who had not regarded the face of El Babooni as a thing of beauty during his lifetime and considered that little or no improvement had been effected by death, thought it highly improbable that this grisly relic could give much pleasure to anyone, but could only suppose the Baron knew best.

By the time the Baron and William had arrived at the space in front of the royal tent where the levée was to be held, a large crowd had already assembled. Thanks, however, to the energy of the Baron and the fact that he had a friend in the Lord Chamberlain's office, they were given very good places in the queue and settled down to wait patiently until their sovereign should emerge.

Exactly on the stroke of ten, with a punctuality which has ever distinguished our Royal House, the trumpets sounded, the guards presented arms, unseen hands whisked apart the flaps of the tent, and His Majesty, King Richard, accompanied by a numerous retinue of chambermaids, secretaries, chaplains, allied commanders and others, advanced to take his seat on the throne which had been placed on a dais opposite the head of the queue. His sovereign's countenance struck William as noble and benign: the blue if slightly prominent eyes formed a pleasing contrast to the red of the beard and hair and the expression was condescending but affable. A rather less pleasing impression, however, was created by the appearance of His Majesty's attendants. William

was an idealistic young man and found it hard altogether to
suppress a feeling of disappointment on his first sight of so many
figures prominent in public life. In those days, you must remember, there were no photographs or newspapers to render familiar
the likenesses of the leading statesmen of the time, and were you
suddenly to be confronted today with the whole Cabinet and the
more important permanent civil servants, having received no
previous hint of their appearance, you would doubtless be no less
shocked than was poor William on this occasion.

But little time was left for reflection on these matters, for
William had hardly recovered from his surprise when he found
himself at the head of the queue being urged forward by the
Baron. As he sank down on one knee, eyes fixed on the ground, he
heard the chamberlain read out his name and titles, and those of
the Baron, which was followed by a short silence broken finally by
a thunderous rasping sound that he did not at once realise was his
Sovereign clearing his throat. This over, he heard the royal voice,
more kindly but hardly less forceful than that of the Dame of
Courantsdair, addressing him in the warmest manner.

'William de Littlehampton. We are doubly pleased to welcome
you among us to-day. First as your father's son; for the late Sir—,
the late Sir—, um the late—' at this point William noticed an

anxious face pop over the top of the throne and whisper hurriedly in the royal ear '—the late Sir Dagobert was among Our Royal Father's most trusted lieges. Second, We welcome you in your own right as one who has accomplished a notable feat of arms, gaining great credit for yourself and affording much assistance to the Holy Cause we are all sword to defend. Some time We would much like to hear from your own lips a full account of your prowess in yesterday's engagement. Now, alas, affairs of state are pressing. However, We cannot take Our leave of so gallant a knight without bestowing some signal mark of Our favour.'

At this a page came forward with a beautiful pair of golden spurs on a cushion which His Majesty took and, with that gracious condescension which had done so much to endear him to all ranks of his subjects, himself fixed them on the feet of the trembling William. Then, taking the immense sword which rested across his knees, he tapped William lightly on the shoulder and said in ringing tones: 'Rise, Sir William.'

So overcome was our hero at this totally unexpected gesture that he would undoubtedly have forgotten to present his own gift had the Baron not jabbed him sharply in the ribs. Blushing furiously, and doing his best to conceal both his distaste for the present and his anxiety as to its reception, he mumbled some quite inaudible words of gratitude and loyalty and laid the bundle at the King's feet.

Sir William need have had no fear for the reaction his gift was to produce, for no sooner had he removed the cloth than a murmur of the most genuine appreciation arose on all sides and there at once appeared in the Royal Eye a look of animation which had up to that moment been quite lacking. Many remarks highly flattering to William's pride and sadly critical of El Babooni's appearance, were passed by those present, and when the relic was removed by an attendant His Majesty gave instructions that it was to be carefully stuffed and mounted and sent back to hang with other remarkable trophies of the chase in the great hall at Windsor.

'Your thoughtful gesture,' said the Monarch, 'in presenting Us with this splendid memento of a notable action has deeply touched Us, and as a small token of Our gratitude, We command that you shall have the honour of carrying Our Royal Standard in the great attack which is to be launched to-morrow. Moreover, We graciously permit you under Our Royal Warrant from henceforth to bear as your badge, crest and ensign a severed Saracen's head proper, and to transmit the same to all your descendants in the male line from generation to generation.'

Thus saying the King rose, indicating that the levée was now at an end, and followed by all his attendants withdrew into his tent.

Sir William was deeply touched by all these marks of the Royal Favour. His golden spurs clinked in a most gratifying fashion and attracted much favourable comment from all his companions, and the thought of at last being able to get rid of Sir Dagobert's old boar's-head on his coat of arms which had throughout his youth proved for him a badge of humiliation, and to replace it with this far more dashing and exotic device, gave him boundless pleasure. The consideration of how much it would annoy his mother did not, I am sorry to say, in any way lessen his satisfaction. With regard to the honourable and eagerly sought-after post of Royal Standard Bearer he was less certain. His responsibilities he realised would be very heavy and he was anxious lest Lillian should prove unable to keep up with the Royal Charger, for he understood it to be his privilege always to be within five paces of the Monarch throughout the day. Moreover, he was distressed by the fear that his sudden elevation to this important post might provoke the jealousy of the previous Standard Bearer whom he did not doubt to be one of the immensely distinguished characters of whom Sir Cuthbert had spoken. So seriously did he consider this possibility that he confided his fears later that day to Sir Cuthbert himself.

'My dear boy, you can set your mind at rest on that score,' de Brett assured him, 'for there is at present no Royal Standard Bearer. The last man to hold the post was poor Odo de Basing-stoke who was killed last Saturday, his first day in office. Before that there was Etienne du Chemin-de-Fer-du-Nord, who died on the previous Wednesday having taken over from Wolfgang von der Bummelzug but three days earlier.'

'Oh,' said William in a rather depressed tone of voice, 'and what happened to Wolfgang von der what d'you call him?'

'He, poor fellow, was laid low by a bow shot right at the end of the engagement. That was the day when there were no less than three different standard bearers in the twenty-hour hours, a record for the whole campaign.'

As William lay awake that night brooding on his conversation with Sir Cuthbert, he came to realise for the first time that one of the great drawbacks of a noble reputation is the strain of keeping it up.

Dawn was still but a faint pinkish glow in the east when William, who had slept very badly, was aroused by sounds of immense activity throughout the camp. Complicated trumpet calls rang out on all sides; the noise of rivetting and swearing in half a dozen languages filled the air as hundreds of knights were assisted into their armour; and the ground shook beneath the pawing and trampling of as many chargers being exercised by grooms and pages. Poor William who seldom felt at his best at this hour of the day, grew increasingly depressed and the eager chatter of Leofric, who was bustling round here, there and everywhere did little to cheer him. Only from the freshly painted Saracen's Head, glowering from his shield, did he gain any comfort.

Arrived at the Royal Tent, William found what appeared to be the utmost confusion reigning. Dashing young staff officers kept leaping on and off horses and dashing away on unspecified errands. Pages and armourers shot in and out with helms, battleaxes, shields and all sorts of equipment, and no-one seemed to have either the leisure or the inclination to tell Sir William where to go or what exactly to do. Accordingly he dismounted, giving his reins to Leofric and remained respectfully as near the door of the tent as he could get – a position in which he caused the maximum inconvenience to everyone.

At last, just as the first rays of the sun shot above the low horizon, a final flurry of staff officers dashed out to announce the immediate appearance of His Majesty and a few seconds later the King himself emerged.

Clad in full armour, though modestly wearing on his surcoat the plain scarlet cross of the Crusader, King Richard having smiled graciously on William, vaulted lightly on to his immense charger that was completely enshrouded in a scarlet saddle-cloth embroidered all over with the royal leopards. Whereupon one nobleman dashed forward to hand him his sword and shield, another lifted up his great helm topped by the Crown of England, while a third thrust into the hands of William, who had only just managed to get mounted in time, the Royal Standard.

Puzzled, uncertain what to do, and dreadfully apprehensive, poor William was delighted suddenly to notice among the crowd the familiar features of the Baron of Barking-West.

'Well, my boy,' said the latter, 'good luck and God be with you. You know what you have to do? Never let the King out of your sight for one moment and never fall more than five paces behind! Don't worry about killing Moslems; the other fellows will do that all right. All you have to do is to keep the flag flying. Goodbye and good luck.'

On that historic day the English contingent, with their Sovereign at their head, occupied the very centre of the Allied line, and even William, nervous as he was, felt his heart beat faster with pride as his eye travelled over the long rows of horsemen, the pennons of their lances stirring gently in the early morning breeze, and the sun gleaming and flashing from their helms and weapons. Immediately in front lay the walls and towers of Acre, but between them and the ramparts was already drawn up the main body of the Saracen host. After an extended study of their position King Richard turned to his trumpeter who blew a long warning blast on his horn that was re-echoed by trumpeters all through the army and, standing in his stirrups, raised aloft his great sword. After what seemed to William an age, but can only have been a few seconds, he waved it three times round his head, the trumpets sounded once more and the whole line moved forward at a brisk trot.

It was not long before the King himself had drawn slightly ahead of the line, and when the pace increased from a trot to a canter and then to a gallop this distance steadily increased. Poor Lillian, who had no great turn of speed, was hard pressed, but seemed fully to realise her great responsibility and, puffing but indomitable, succeeded in keeping the regulation five paces behind. William, recalling the fact that, encumbered with the great standard, he would have to look to others for his defence, felt this isolation from the main body very keenly. However, he had little time for such sombre reflections before he found himself, as it were in a flash, in the midst of the tumult. One moment the ferocious Moslem soldiery seemed to be a good quarter of a mile ahead; the next they were all around him and on every side.

Of all the fearful details of that heroic day Sir William could later recall but few. Nobly, but only with difficulty, following his Sovereign he was throughout in the very thick of the fighting. Swords and battleaxes rose and fell, heads and limbs rolled on the ground, lances shivered and arrows whizzed all around him. Twice an arrow pierced his surcoat, and no less than twelve found their mark on his bright new shield. Poor Lillian's energies began to flag half-way through, but fortunately an arrow in the rump livened her up to an astonishing degree. At last quite suddenly they found themselves at the foot of the walls and all the great host, which a short time before had been drawn up below, had vanished away leaving a trail of dead and wounded behind them. Whereupon the King, regardless of the arrows and stones which were still whistling down from the battlements, gave the order to dismount and called in a loud voice for scaling ladders. As soon as these had been set against the walls he advanced briskly to the nearest, closely followed by William, and started to mount.

While the Royal Foot was yet on the lower rungs a terrible thing happened. William, in his fear of being left behind, dashed heedlessly forward, slipped in a pool of blood, and fell flat on his back. At that very moment there leapt from the ground, where he had been feigning death in the hope of such a chance as William's mishap now offered, a repellent Arab clutching a long knife which he raised, snarling with savage glee, high above the prostrate Standard Bearer. William had given himself up for lost and was fumbling desperately for his shield, on which in fact he was sitting, when suddenly there was a growl and dirty yellow flash, and Charlemagne, tailless but unhesitating, flung himself at the Infidel's throat. Regretfully, but knowing well his duty, William scrambled to his feet clutching tight the Standard and dashed up the ladder after the King, leaving poor Charlemagne to his fate.

How William ever reached the top of that ladder he never knew. He had never had a good head for heights and quite apart from the shaking and quivering caused by the weight of two knights in full armour hurrying up it as quick as they could, there was a hail of stones, arrows, and humble but familiar pieces of crockery hurled down by the defenders above.

Somehow, however, he managed to survive and in what seemed a remarkable short space of time, the Christian watchers below sent up cheer upon cheer. There, silhouetted against the bright blue sky on the very highest section of the walls were visible the stalwart figure of the Lionheart waving his sword in triumph alongside the Royal Standard firmly planted on the battlements and guarded by Sir William de Littlehampton. While round their feet there gambolled, barking triumphantly, a tailless wolfhound whose unattractive appearance was for once redeemed by a justified self-assurance.

CHAPTER 5

The Home-Coming

HE sun was blazing from a cloudless sky and had it not been for a slight sea-breeze, just sufficient to fill the sails of the *Santa Caterina Lachrymosa*, the heat would have been intolerable. Stretched out in the shadow of the poop lay William, fanned by the faithful Hercule, eating dates and observing with interest a flying fish that was careering from wave to wave alongside the ship.

Some six weeks had passed since the fall of Acre and with the advance of summer the campaigning season had drawn to a close. Many of the Crusaders felt that although Jerusalem remained in the hands of the infidel enough had been accomplished to justify their departure. This feeling was shared by William who, moreover, considered that to stay longer would be to tempt Providence, for luck such as his could not surely continue indefinitely. On learning therefore that a large, fast ship was leaving shortly from Tyre for Marseilles, he had booked a passage to the latter port with the intention of continuing his journey overland to the Channel.

They had now been some three days at sea and although the coast of Syria lay far behind they had remained in sight of numerous small islands, one of which at this moment lay a couple of leagues to starboard. William was just enquiring of Hercule what land it was when there came from the look-out the familiar cry, 'A sail, a sail!'

The reaction produced by this warning was very different from that which has occured on board the *St Caradoc*; the *Santa Caterina Lachrymosa* was a far larger vessel, heavily armed, and thanks to her two banks of oars manned by well-whipped galleyslaves, had a great turn of speed, and those who bothered to mount the poop to gaze in the direction indicated by the look-out did so from idle curiosity rather than apprehension. The sail in question turned out to be a small galley which sheered off as soon as she had sighted their own ship, and William, after a casual glance, returned to his contemplation of the flying fish.

At first the elusive creature seemed completely to have disappeared, but at length William discerned a gleam in the waves some few yards to port. What was his astonishment to realise as he looked closer that this was not his old acquaintance but a glass bottle! His curiosity fully aroused by so unusual a sight (glass bottles were not then the commonplace articles they are today), he turned to Charlemagne, who lay panting by his side, saying 'Go on then, fetch it, boy!' Charlemagne, by no means loath to take a dip and eager to show off his prowess in the water, cleared the bulwark at one bound, swam rapidly towards the bottle, gripped it firmly between his teeth and with some difficulty and a little assistance from a kindly sailor with a boat-hook, regained the deck.

On examing the bottle, which Charlemagne had laid obediently at his feet, William was interested to observe that it contained a small roll of parchment which, on extraction, proved to be covered in writing that he assumed to be Greek. Fortunately Hercule had been at one time in the Byzantine service and was well acquainted with the Greek tongue. Accordingly on his master's bidding he translated the document as follows.

> *If you be Christians in that great vesssel, take pity, I beg you, on a young maiden of gentle birth, cruelly kidnapped from her native land, who is even now being carried away by Infidel pirates to slavery and a fate worse than death.*
>
> DESPINA PROTOPAPPADOPOULOS.

On hearing this cry of anguish William was deeply distressed. He was most anxious to reach Marseilles with all possible speed and reluctant to suffer any delay, but he was now, he remembered, a knight and he had read a quite sufficient number of romances to realise that the rescue of maidens in distress was from henceforth to be one of his principal lines of business. With as good a grace, therefore, as he could achieve, he summoned the Master, explained to him the obligation under which he rested and asked for the ship to be turned about in hot pursuit of the galley which was even now disappearing over the horizon.

Almost at once the rhythm of the oars redoubled in speed as the whips cracked across the shoulders of the unfortunate gal-leyslaves. At the same time, as if Providence approved of William's unselfish decision, the breeze quickened and in a very short space it became clear that the *Santa Caterina Lachrymosa* was rapidly gaining on her quarry. This, it seemed, was as obvious aboard the galley as it was to William and his companions, for the pirates suddenly changed course and ran into the shallow waters in the lee of the small island where they obviously judged the larger vessel would be unable to follow. However, terror made them careless, and a sudden reduction in speed followed by a long rending sound, clearly audible across the water, announced that they had hit a rock. The vessel almost at once began to founder and the pirates were observed to be diving overboard in large numbers and swimming rapidly towards the shore. Then, just a split second before the galley sank, a small figure clad in white was seen to run up the deck and, with a gesture of infinite pathos, cast herself into the waves from that side of the ship opposite the *Santa Caterina Lachrymosa*.

Once more William found himself in an intolerable dilemma. Their ship, it was obvious, could not safely get more closely inshore, there was no dinghy and a brief enquiry made it clear that of the ship's company only William and Leofric could swim. Much as he disliked that form of exercise William saw clearly that he would have to plunge in, for to allow Leofric to get away with the credit alone would be unthinkable. Accordingly, drawing some comfort from the reflection that the Mediterranean was unlikely to prove so cold as the moat of Courantsdair, he jumped briskly over the side, calling upon Leofric to follow.

William's efforts were fully rewarded for, by dint of quite extraordinary exertions, he reached the maiden's side just as she was going down for the third time, and with the assistance of Leofric, and despite the well-meaning, but on the whole ineffective, efforts of Charlemagne to be of use, succeeded in bringing her to the *Santa Caterina Lachrymosa*.

After the whole party had dried in the sun the unfortunate maiden who had been afforded such comforts as the ship could provide, was prevailed upon through the medium of Hercule to tell her story. She was, it appeared, the only daughter of Constantine Protopappadopoulos, Lord of the island of Kolynos. She had, but two days previously, been playing blindman's buff with her girl friends on the seashore close to her home, when a band of corsairs suddenly sprang out from behind a rock. She, unfortunately, had been 'he,' and assuming the screams of her companions, who had fled at the first sight of the intruders, to be all part of the game, had run blindfolded into the arms of her captors.

Deeply moved by this touching recital, as were all the ship's company, William saw clearly that there was nothing for it but to turn aside to Kolynos, which fortunately the Master assured him was but a day's sail to starboard, and restore the unfortunate girl to the arms of her father.

Early next morning a cry from aloft informed William that they were in sight of the island of Kolynos and natural curiosity to see the home of the beautiful Despina prompted him to go at once to the poop. The view which met his eyes was quite unexpectedly rewarding; there rose up from the sea, about two leagues ahead, a great mountain whose sides seemed to drop almost perpendicularly to the water's edge. To the east, however, there jutted out a short arm of comparatively flat land, fringed on one side with a long strip of sandy beach backed by palms, caribs, figs and olives, and on the other by numerous buildings in a most refined style of architecture facing a considerable harbour enclosed by a fortified mole of well-constructed masonry. On the very top of the mountain there appeared a great castle of apparently miraculous construction, connected with the town below by a long flight of steps curling and backing up the mountain-side, protected at intervals by castellated gateways and formidable curtain-walls.

However, the air of gaiety and charm which the town possessed when seen from a distance proved on closer view to be largely

illusory. All the shops along the sea-front were shut, the ships in the harbour had their flags at half-mast, and from the domed church behind the houses came the sound of gloomy chanting. Despite the bright colour of many of the buildings, the sparkling waters of the harbour and the brilliant sunlight in which the whole scene was bathed, an indescribable air of depression hung about the entire place.

At first the waterside appeared to be completely deserted, but at length, just after they had lowered the gangplank, a solitary customs official, of infinitely depressed appearance, sauntered gloomily towards them, and as William, courteously giving his arm to Miss Protopappadopoulos, appeared at the side, asked in hollow tones to see their passports.

As William was quite unacquainted with the Greek tongue it was his fair companion who replied, and at the sound of her voice the official condescended to raise his eyes from the ground for the first time. Instantly his face was transfigured, his eyes almost popped from their sockets, a radiant but incredulous smile lightened his countenance and falling on his knees he covered Despina's hands with kisses. Almost at once further figures, attracted by the sounds of the customs official's rejoicing, appeared from the neighbouring houses, and as the news of their lady's return spread like wildfire through the town the whole atmosphere completely changed. Shutters were taken down from the shops, the sound of chanting stopped abruptly to be succeeded by the ringing of church bells, and from every street and alley radiant Greeks poured onto the quayside to swell the vast crowd by which William and Despina were already surrounded.

So over-excited were the loyal and affectionate townspeople that there is no saying when William and Despina would have been disentangled had they been left to their own devices, but it was not long before the crowd fell back to make way for a distinguished group of newcomers rapidly approaching down the hill from the direction of the Castle. At the head of the little procession was a nobleman of refined and venerable appearance, clad in a style far richer than that affected by the upper classes of society in England. William at once assumed him to be the Lord of Kolynos – an assumption that was almost immediately confirmed by the old man's enfolding Despina in his arms while the tears coursed down their cheeks. After some minutes during which

relief and joy bereft both parent and child of speech, Despina, talking at great speed, explained to her father the circumstances of her rescue and led him up to the slightly embarrassed William. In excellent French, of which the fluency was only slightly impaired by strong emotion, the good old man expressed at length his gratitude, admiration and wonder and finally concluded a speech, the length of which was agreeably enlivened by a wealth of gesture, by insisting that William and his page should immediately accompany him to his castle while the rest of the ship's company were to be entertained at the public charge by the delighted citizens.

The palace of the Lord of Kolynos, for castle was too austere a term to describe so magnificent a dwelling, quite overwhelmed William by the convenience of its arrangements and the luxury of its furnishings. The walls were adorned with exquisite views of noble buildings and elegantly designed landscapes, all carried out in the most beautiful mosaic. In one room Adam and Eve were seen in the Garden of Eden surrounded by every known species of flower and shrub, and beautifully rendered animals of an unquestionable docility. In another the great Achilles was riding at speed round the walls of Troy, dragging behind him the body of Hector, and observed with deep emotion by Priam and Helen clearly distinguishable on the battlements above. The floors of the innumerable apartments were all inlaid with marble and covered, in some cases, by magnificent carpets of oriental workmanship;

and through open doorways one caught sight of cool loggias laid out with potted shrubs and refreshed by ingeniously designed fountains. It was all, William felt, very unlike Courantsdair.

Such were the comforts and wonders of Kolynos that William, despite his anxiety to get home as quickly as possible, could hardly bear to put an end to his stay beneath Constantine Protopappadopoulos' hospitable roof. In particular he acquired a great fondness for Turkish baths, with which the castle was bountifully supplied, and of which he had previously never so much as heard. However, at the end of a week, despite the sincere and voluble protests of both Despina and her father, he firmly announced that the wind being favourable he must depart at sunrise the next day. When the Lord of Kolynos saw that nothing he could say would shake the determination of his guest, he reluctantly consented to his departure, announcing at the same time that there would take place the same night a farewell banquet which all the ship's company, together with the most distinguished residents of the island, were without fail to attend.

To catalogue the innumerable dishes which were set before William, or to describe their exquisite flavour, or the refined manner of their preparation is a task beyond my powers. I can only tell you that the great feast in El Babooni's stronghold seemed in retrospect to have been little better than a provincial bean-feast, and, in comparison with the elegance and subtlety of this menu, to have been characterised solely by an ostentatious and vulgar profusion. However, even the most ingenious of repasts must some time come to an end, and at length, when the last fruits had been removed, the glasses finally recharged, the Lord of Kolynos rose to take leave of his guest in a speech which William expected to be long, but little guessed would have so dramatic a close.

'Loyal subjects and distinguished guests,' said Constantine Protopappadopoulos, 'we are met together this evening to bid farewell to one who by his valour and resource has laid the whole island, and particularly its ruler, under an obligation which can never properly be discharged. Of the circumstances and occasion of his coming among us you are fully aware, and there is no need therefore for me to enlarge upon them, even had I the fluency and descriptive powers properly to do so.'

Nevertheless for the next twenty minutes the good old man proceeded to describe in detail every aspect of his daughter's plight and her miraculous delivery, adding several exciting incidents such as an underwater fight with the leader of the pirates and a breathless pursuit by man-eating sharks, of which William, to tell the truth, had very little clear recollection.

'And now, my friends,' continued their host, 'how best may we recompense this heroic and incomparable young man? I confess I have spent long and sleepless nights in debating just this question and only now have I found an answer which, however painful it may be to me personally, I am convinced provides the only solution.'

At this point in the speech there came into the host's voice a note of deep emotion, and he paused to cast a glance of inexpressible tenderness towards his only child.

'Old as I am, my eyesight is still good, and I have not failed to notice this last few days the warmth and affection in the glances which my beloved daughter has freely bestowed upon our young visitor. He for his part, with that gentlemanly reserve which so distinguishes the gallant race from which he springs, has done his best to conceal his true feelings beneath a mask of stoical indifference. But I was not deceived! My daughter is, as you well know, the light of my life and the apple of my eye, but nevertheless deeply and long as I shall miss her – and here I think I am speaking not only for myself but for all loyal Kolynotes – her happiness must always be my first consideration.

'Take her, dear boy, take her,' he cried, turning to William with the tears pouring down his cheeks, 'and may she ever prove as loyal a wife as she has been dutiful a daughter.'

Poor William was too embarrassed to speak and was, moreover, very much afraid that he was going to have hiccups. What on earth would his mother say if he were to come back with a foreign bride? Whatever was he going to do about Gertrude? And then, as the memory of Gertrude's weather-beaten features and huntin' voice came to him afresh and he looked across the table at Despina, whose beauty had indeed made a deep, if unconscious impression, his mind was suddenly made up. Rising to his feet he crossed the hall and took both the hands of the lovely heiress in his own.

*   *   *

The sun was low above the western downs and, although it still wanted two days till the harvest was in, there was already a feeling of approaching autumn in the air. A faint mist was gathering in the meadows below the castle, mingling with the wood smoke rising from the village hidden from sight in the valley. In the bailey, across which the shadow of the great keep was slowly extending, a large hay-wain was being unloaded alongside the stables, the castle cat was stretching in that corner of the gatehouse which still retained the sun, and a row of ducklings went quacking in the wake of the gatehouse-keeper's daughter carrying a pot of mash to the pigsty. High above this peaceful scene in a sheltered corner of the battlements, the Dame de Courantsdair was watering her potted plants.

Nearly a year had gone by since William's departure for the Crusade and during all that time no word had reached Courantsdair. Local rumour had it that Sir Willibald de Wandsworth had been slain, but no details of his tragic end had as yet come to the ears of his neighbours. The Dame, although she would have died rather than admit it, was growing nervous, and her youngest daughter Gwendolen, William's favourite sister, made no effort to conceal her anxiety and was even now on the topmost turret of the keep scanning the road to the sea. This look-out she had recently made her daily charge at this hour of the evening, but was today observing every detail of the distant scene with a more than usual absorption. For Abbot Slapjack, who had arrived at the castle late the previous evening had announced the presence of a large vessel from foreign parts lying out in the roads and the fond girl hoped against hope that some messenger might be aboard bringing tidings of her beloved brother. The Abbot himself, not a sentimental type, attached little importance to his own news, and was comfortably installed in the Dame's solar composing his sermon for the forthcoming Harvest Festival.

The Dame had just emptied her watering-can and was preparing to go indoors when a shrill scream from aloft drew her attention to her daughter who was pointing with wild excitement towards the coast road. Almost despite herself the formidable matron cast a glance in the same direction, and as she did so the sharp reprimand which Gwendolen was about to receive on the rudeness of 'pointing,' died on her lips.

Coming over the crest of the hill, just before where the road sank once more from sight of the village below, was an impressive procession.

First came a gigantic negro, superbly mounted, carrying a large banner with an unfamiliar device, closely followed by a snub-nosed youth whom Gwendolen, whose eyesight was sharper than her mother's, was hysterically certain was Leofric. Then came a closed litter borne on the backs of two mules alongside which rode a handsome youth on a grey mare whom the Dame for some time remained unconvinced was really her son, and at whose heels there gambolled a large, tailless hound of familiar ugliness. Behind were visible two men-at-arms and a long string of servants and pack animals.

By the time the tail of the procession had passed over the brow of the hill, the negro and Leofric, were already clattering over the drawbridge into the outer bailey, and a sound of cheering from the village announced that the loyal villeins had recognised their returning lord. The scene which now took place in the courtyard was indescribably affecting. The gatehouse-keeper, the gate-house-keeper's wife, the gatehouse-keeper's daughter, and the gatehouse-keeper's dog made no effort to conceal their emotion and the behaviour of Gwendolen and her six sisters was hardly more restrained. Only the Dame maintained her usual well-bred, unruffled calm, but even on that stern and dignified countenance a close observer might have noticed, if the truth were told, a faint tremor at the corner of the determined mouth, a hint of dampness in the eagle eye.

Sir William, for his part, was deeply moved by the warmth of his reception and embraced his sisters with a genuine affection and his mother with a respectful tenderness. Nevertheless those who knew him best might possibly have detected a slight shade of nervousness in his manner. This, however, completely vanished on his overhearing one of his sisters remark with an engaging innocence how sorry poor Gertrude would be to miss this home-coming, and how ill she had timed her visit to her aunt the Abbess. Thereupon his brow cleared and with a firm determined step he advanced to the closed litter, which had already aroused the keenest speculation among the bystanders, and drawing back the curtains assisted Despina to alight saying in loud, unshaken tones, as he did so, 'Mother, I wish to present to you the Lady de Littlehampton.'

The stunned silence which greeted this announcement was finally broken by the astounded Dame.

'But, but – Gertrude?' she said.

'She can go into a nunnery,' Sir William easily replied, adding a little unkindly, 'she was everlastingly saying she felt she had a call to the religious life. And now,' he continued quickly before anyone had time to discuss the point, 'we will go in and tidy. Then in half an hour all will repair to the Chapel where Abbot Slapjack, whom I am delighted to see here today, will celebrate our nuptials.'

Noticing the look of consternation which came over his mother's face at this announcement, Sir William made haste to explain that as the previous ceremony had been conducted according to the rites of the Greek Orthodox Church, he had thought it as well to repeat them on his return.

'After that,' he went on, 'there will be a wedding feast in the great hall, which some of my people here,' indicating with a casual wave of his hand the long retinue of servants, 'will take steps to prepare while we are in the Chapel.' So saying he took Despina by the hand, whom, after she had made a deep curtsey to the Dame, he led into the Castle.

The wedding ceremony, conducted by the Abbot with all his usual mastery, was simple but touching. The bride, in an exquisite white gown of a material which was quite unfamiliar to the ladies of Courantsdair and which they were interested to learn was called silk, looked ravishing. The bridegroom, whose beautiful golden spurs attracted much attention, seemed to have acquired a new confidence and dignity. And it was generally agreed that for once no fault could be found even with the behaviour of Leofric.

It was a late hour, indeed, before anyone in the castle retired to bed that night. Over and over again William was forced to recount every detail of his journey and adventures, which he did with a becoming modesty and, all things considered, remarkable accuracy. On only one point did he in any way diverge from the strictest truth. In explaining the loss of poor Charlemagne's tail he gave the company to understand that this had occurred in the gallant action beneath the walls of Acre. At long last, after he had described for the fifteenth time his overthrow of El Babooni, had recounted word for word his interview with his sovereign, and had distributed the last of the costly and exotic gifts with which he had come laden from Kolynos, he rose, bidding his mother and sisters a fond night, took Despina by the hand, and gave the signal for a general departure to bed.

*   *   *

In the years which followed the events recounted in this story the respect and affection in which Sir William and his lady were held by all who knew them steadily increased, and the castle of Courantsdair, in which its owner had effected many improvements – glass in the windows, Persian rugs on the floors, rich frescoes on the walls, and many other luxuries which, although common enough in the East were totally unfamiliar in Sussex – became famous throughout the length and breadth of the land for its hospitality and high standard of living.

The Dame in the course of time was gathered to her fathers at the ripe age of eighty-eight; her daughters remained single, with the exception of Gwendolen, who married Leofric less than a year after William's return; and Gertrude in due course succeeded her aunt as Abbess of a neighbouring convent, where her filthy temper and unnatural strictness made life intolerable for all the nuns. Charlemagne lived to a ripe old age, much respected by all the dogs of the neighbourhood and the terror of every puppy for miles around. Hercule in due course married the gatehouse-keeper's daughter, and their union was blessed with nine children, three white, three black, and three piebald.

Today more than seven centuries have passed since all these things took place and small trace now remains of any of the figures in this tale. The ruins of the castle of Courantsdair were long conspicuous, but were finally sold by the father of the present Lord Littlehampton some years ago in order to pay death duties, and the site is now covered by the Chateau Housing Estate. Today the only remaining indication of that once formidable pile is to be found in Nos. 18 to 25 Acacia Road which, being rather hastily erected on the side of the old moat, are quite exceptionally damp in winter.

In the little village church of Currants the beautiful tomb of William and Despina, in the early Gothic style, is still preserved alongside that of Sir Dagobert although rather overshadowed by the white marble resting-place (adorned with sixteen cherubs, a life-size statue of the deceased in a full-bottom wig and allegorical figures of Faith, Hope and Charity) of his eighteenth-century descendant, Admiral of the Blue, Sir Marmaduke Little-hampton.*

Of the village which William knew as a boy no trace at all remains. Nevertheless, if you look up above the door of the ancient inn (almost completely modernised in recent years), that long ago replaced *The Blue Boar* which occupied the site in the time of Sir Dagobert, you will still see, weatherbeaten, but recognisable, creaking rustily beneath the eaves, the proud sign of *The Saracen's Head.*

* Strangely enough still unrecorded even by Mrs Esdaile.

FINIS

DRAYNEFLETE
REVEALED

Contents

Notes on Illustrations

The illustrations on pp. 115, 149 are reproduced by kind permission of the Earl of Littlehampton: those on pp. 105, 109, 119, 120, 121, 130, 138 by kind permission of the Curator and Trustees of the Drayneflete Art Gallery: those on pp. 124, 128, by kind permission of Miss Dracula Parsley-ffigett. The reconstructions of historic Drayneflete were specially drawn for the present work and are founded on the results of the most recent archaeological research collated, in the later examples, with contemporary prints and photographs.

The wood-engraving of the old North Gate on the title-page is taken from *Picturesque Walks in Drayneflete and its Environs described by a Lady of Title* (London, 1852).

Preface

So generally is the importance of local histories now realised that an author need make no apology for adding to their number. It was indeed a matter of some astonishment to discover that the history of a town so well known as Drayneflete, with so rich and yet so typical a past, should have been left so long unrecorded, and it was therefore with some sense of mission that I set about my present task.

The local authorities, rightly anxious to stimulate the tourist trade and fully intending that their town should play its proper role in the forthcoming Festival of Britain, afforded every assistance and encouragement and I therefore welcome this opportunity of acknowledging my indebtedness. In particular I should like to mention Miss Runcorn, the Municipal Librarian, ever ready to transcribe original documents in her keeping; Mr Soames, the learned and genial curator of the Drayneflete museum and art gallery; and Canon Stavely-Locker and the Churchwardens of St Ermintrude's, to whose kindness I am indebted not only for permission to reproduce various monuments in the Church, but for much curious and valuable information.

Others without whose assistance this work could never have been brought to a successful conclusion are Maud, Countess of Littlehampton, whose kind interest and charming sympathy added so much to the pleasures of research; Miss Dracula Parlsey-ffigett, who proved a veritable mine of extraordinary information which could have been obtained from no other source; the Hon Mervyn Horder for so kindly drawing my attention to the tune printed on page 102, of the existence of which I should otherwise have remained totally unaware; Mr John Piper for his advice on syntax; and finally to my dear wife who undertook the arduous task of proof-reading.

[85]

Pre-Conquest Drayneflete

Few towns in England can boast so long a continuous history as Drayneflete. From the earliest times human habitations of one sort or another have clustered along the north bank of the River Drayne at the highest point where this shallow but treacherous stream is easily fordable. Or perhaps even earlier, for it is conceivable, though admittedly there is little to suggest it, that primitive man dwelt here before even there was a river at all, at a time when France and England were joined by a land-bridge and vast mammoths and sabre-toothed tigers prowled through the tropical undergrowth where now stands Marks and Spencers.

However that may be, we do know that early in the Bronze Age Drayneflete was already an important settlement on the great trackway from the Thames to the coast that has been known at various times as Wiggling Way, the Via Hernia and A999. Interesting evidence of the high level of 'the Drayneflete culture' (as it has come to be known) was afforded by the discovery of a long barrow some years ago during the rebuilding of the Fever Hospital on Drayneflete Down. Workmen, little realising the importance of their treasure-trove, unearthed some broken pots, a string of beads and a quantity of clay cylinders of undetermined

Contents of a long barrow opened on Drayneflete Down in 1888, now in the Museum. From a drawing by Miss Catnip, published in the 'Proceedings of the Drayneflete Archaeological Society', Vol. XXXII.

purpose, all lying mingled with a quantity of human bones. The find was immediately recorded (see the *Proceedings of the Drayneflete Archaeological Society*, Volume XXXII, pp. 85–97), but it was not until the various objects had been submitted to the expert analysis of Professor Spiggot of London University and Dr Flackenbacker of Yale, that their full significance was realised. For the layman it may seem almost incredible that so full a picture can be built up on so slight a foundation, but modern methods of laboratory research now enable archaeologists to speak with an assurance that would have astonished their predecessors. Lack of space prevents us from describing the complicated and laborious methods of enquiry employed by the Professors and we can only summarise their conclusions.

The occupant of the grave was, it appears, a local chieftain, middle-aged, five foot seven in height and markedly dolicho-cephalic. He was married, but not happy in his home life, suffered from stomach ulcers and an impacted wisdom tooth and died as a result of a sharp blow over the left ear. He had probably fallen on his head as a child and was certainly devoted to his dog, a cross-bred mastiff, eight hands in height with a badly damaged tail. The pottery was hand-turned of a fairly common type indicative of cultural contacts with the lower Meuse and probably did not hold water. The beads were imported from the Baltic and subject to a heavy purchase-tax which indicates that the Drayneflete com-munity was comparatively wealthy. The clay cylinders of very peculiar shape were at one time thought to be primitive lace-bobbins, but as there is no evidence of lace-making at this early date Professor Flackenbacker is probably correct in saying that they played an important part in some fertility rite.

The Romans, when they came, were not slow to realise the importance of the site and a large garrison town, Dra-conobododum, was soon established on the north bank. Innumer-able discoveries made in the course of the huge-scale building development of the last twenty years have enabled us to form a fairly clear picture of the life and appearance of the town at this date, which would seem to have been of considerable size and importance. There was a temple of Castor and Pollux occupying the site of the present Parish Church, large baths situated roughly at the corner of the market square and Littlehampton Street, and another temple standing on ground now covered by the offices of

the Drayneflete and District Electric Light Co, that was probably
dedicated to the worship of Venus Suburbia, the Suburban
Aphrodite, a cult very popular in Roman Britain. In the centre of
the market square there stood a gigantic statue of an Emperor, of
which the head (now in the Museum) was discovered by a Mr
Brickworth in 1885 when clearing out an old cesspool in the
Vicarage garden.

Gigantic head of an Emperor
(Claudius? Caligula? Nero?
Trajan? Vespasian?), discovered in
1885 in the Vicarage Garden,
now in the Museum.

In 1907 there were excavated the remains of a Roman villa at
South Drayneflete which have been carefully preserved and can
be viewed by the public on application to the custodian (Rosebud
Cottage, Shinwell Lane). The plumbing arrangements, of great
ingenuity and luxury, are well worth inspection and convey a very
vivid idea of the high standard of living prevailing in the Roman
Provinces in the second century AD. There are also numerous
fragments of mosaic pavements, including one of Leda and the
Swan which is only shown to visitors on the production of a permit
obtainable at the Town Hall.

Whether or not Christianity flourished in Roman Drayneflete is
not clear, but we can hardly refuse to believe that there was a
Christian community, small, doubtless, but correspondingly
devout, established by the end of the second century. However,
the theory, stoutly held by certain interested parties, that the

Roman Drayneflete

Primitive Methodist Chapel in Station Road is built on the site of an early Christian basilica, has little evidence to support it and should be accepted with caution.

Exactly when, or why, the last Roman legions withdrew from Draconobododum we do not know, nor how soon after their departure the town fell a prey to marauding Saxons or Angles (or even possibly Jutes), but we do know, from the evidence provided by excavation, that the town was completely destroyed by fire, probably early in the fifth century.

The first literary mention of Drayneflete occurs in the Chronicle at a date about a century later than the sack. According to the monkish chronicler it was at Drayneflete that Filthfroth the Brisling was baptised together with all his house-carls by St Eggfrith, an event that is charmingly commemorated in the north aisle of the present church by a stained-glass window, the work of Sir Edwin Burne-Jones, presented in 1898 by Miss Wicker in memory of her brother Colonel Wicker who fell in the second Zulu War. The actual circumstances of the conversion of this powerful ruler are the subject of a delightful legend which gained for the town an enviable reputation as a place of pilgrimage throughout the Middle Ages.

Filthfroth, say the chroniclers, was passing through the town on his way to raid the men of Wessex, and, being very tired, decided to pass the night in the great hall of the local thane. Now it so happened that in the household of this thane was a little girl who, quite unknown to her parents, was already a Christian. No sooner had the whole of Filthfroth's household lain down to sleep, than the small child started to recite the 119th Psalm. Now in those days, of course, there were no separate bedrooms and the whole household and all the travellers were passing the night on the floor of the Great Hall. This circumstance naturally rendered the little convert's devotions rather disturbing for her companions and when she had finally come to the end of her song of praise only immediately to start again at the beginning, Filthfroth angrily demanded that she should be immediately silenced. This, however, proved to be easier said than done: in vain was the determined child ordered, entreated, threatened, bullied and finally beaten. Still her little voice rang out. At last, at three o'clock in the morning she revealed that her tongue could only be stilled by the immediate baptism of the Brisling and all his household.

Accordingly a message was at once sent to St Eggfrith, who fortunately was dwelling in a hermitage close by, and just as dawn was breaking Filthfroth, the thane and all their followers were received into the Church, whereupon the little missionary, worn out by her efforts, immediately expired. So moved were the whole company by this event that Filthfroth then and there commanded that a church should be built which was consecrated less than a year later, and where beneath the High Altar the bones of little St Ermintrude, for such was the child's name, were piously interred.

Of this Saxon church virtually nothing remains today, although it is possible that the traces of long-and-short work at the base of the tower may have survived from this date, but in the churchyard there stood (until 1910 when it was removed to the Museum) the broken shaft of a Saxon cross that may well have been contemporary with St Ermintrude's church. The decoration of this monument is of peculiar interest as exhibiting a mingling of classical and Scandinavian motifs unique at this date and has been made the subject of a monograph by Professor Hjalmar Hjalmarsen of Upsala published in the *Jahrbuch für frühchristliche Kunstwissenschaft.*

Saxon cross formerly in the churchyard, now in Museum.

Apart from the cross the only other remains of Saxon Drayneflete are a collection of coins, pots, two broken sword shafts, and a copper dish, probably of Byzantine workmanship, engraved with a view of a domed building, possibly St Sophia, and bearing the legend A PRESENT FROM CONSTANTINOPLE in Greek, which was discovered on the sewage farm some years ago and is known as the 'Drayneflete Hoard'.

However, we should not assume from the comparative paucity of the existing evidence that Drayneflete was a place of small importance in Saxon times. On the contrary contemporary references, though few, all point to its being a flourishing centre of commerce and religion, and we know that at least one Anglo-Saxon monarch, Ethelred the Unready, held his court Moot in the town on two separate occasions. Moreover, late in the ninth century it was the scene of important ecclesiastical events when the Synod of Drayneflete was held in the Church: the Synod at which, it will be recalled, the vexed question of whether or not deacons should be allowed to wear beards without moustaches was finally decided, not, alas, without bloodshed, in favour of Bishop Bolfric and the compulsory moustaches party.

A very few years after these important events, the whole town was destroyed by the Vikings who, under the command of Old Ekdal (or the Wild Duck as he was sometimes called after the device at his masthead) sailed up the Drayne, burnt the church and put all the inhabitants to the sword. Recovery after this disaster was slow, and Drayneflete had not long risen from her ashes when Norman William overthrew Saxon Harold and ushered in the Middle Ages.

Drayneflete Canonicorum

The development of Drayneflete during the Middle Ages was inseparably bound up with that of the institutions of the Church, and the most prominent remaining monuments of this age are all, as elsewhere, ecclesiastical. At the time of the Conquest there already existed a stone-built church, dedicated, curiously enough, to St Sorbo, a saint of whom virtually nothing is known, but whose name has been thought by some to indicate a Celtic origin, while others have attempted to identify him (or her) with St Sambo, a holy man alleged to have been popular in Asia Minor in the first century and traditionally held to have been the Ethiopian eunuch baptised by St Philip. This church which had replaced the one built by Filthfroth (probably destroyed in Viking raids) was itself superseded by a new structure in the Norman style erected towards the end of the eleventh century. All that now remains of the pre-Conquest shrine is the base of the west tower and one Saxon window of two lights of rude and primitive workmanship.

*An interesting old corbel
(late-fourteenth century)
in the south aisle
of the Parish Church.*

Drayneflete immediately after the Norman Conquest

The Norman church consisted of a single aisle and a chancel with a rounded apse. At the very end of the thirteenth century a further rebuilding took place: the south wall was pierced to form an arcade of pointed arches rising on clustered shafts giving on to the new aisle, and the chancel was rebuilt in its present form with an east window of three pointed lancets. A little more than a century later new windows in a style midway between Decorated and Perpendicular were inserted in the south aisle and shortly afterwards a further two stories were added to the tower which, when completed, with an openwork balustrade and pinnacles in the Perpendicular style, must have made a very striking addition to all views of the town. Unfortunately 'Lord Littlehampton's Stump', as it was popularly called locally, did not long survive, being totally destroyed in the great storm of 1608. The beautiful south porch, which happily still exists, dates from a few years later. After the close of the Middle Ages one further addition was made to the church in the shape of the north aisle erected by Sir Pompey Fidgett to accommodate his family tombs in the debased and degraded Gothic of the early seventeenth century. Of the inspired restoration carried out by Sir Gilbert Scott, when many hideous eighteenth-century additions were removed and the whole fabric regained its pristine beauty, I shall speak in the proper place.

The parish church, however, was neither the sole nor the most prominent ecclesiastical building in the town. Late in the thirteenth century a house of Augustinian Canons was established on the banks of the Drayne just outside the North Gate, which continued to flourish and expand up to the time of the Dissolution. Today, alas, all that remains is the exquisite Gateway at the north-east corner of the Market Place known as Prior Bloodwort's Lodging, with its great panelled solar above the archway, now occupied by the offices of the Regional Petroleum Officer. Prior Bloodwort, of whom a life-like statue, now in the Museum, stood in the niche to the west of the arch until it was removed to make way for the present traffic-lights in 1935, played a prominent role in the local history. On traditionally bad terms with the townsmen he gained their undying hatred by appropriating, in addition to the rights of ullage, socage and *jus primae noctis* (exercised, naturally, by a lay deputy), the tolls on the bridge over the River Drayne. Against this unwarrantable extension of the Church's claims the townspeople long protested in vain, and it was not until they were

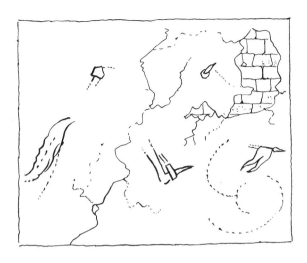

A fifteenth-century wall-painting of St George over the
arcading of the north aisle of the Parish Church.
The first plate shows the state of the painting at the time of its
accidental discovery during repairs to bomb damage in 1944;
the second, after a tactful cleaning by Professor Isolde.

Fifteenth-century Drayneflete

in a position to inform against him to the High Sheriff that he was eventually undone. Unfortunately for him he was unable to answer charges that he had illegally suppressed a prosecution for short-weight baking against a local firm in return for a consideration, and although it was never proved that he received any more than a pork-pasty and half a bottle of sack, he was removed from his office by the Chancellor of the Diocese.

Prior Bloodwort's Lodging, although the sole architectural, is not the only remaining treasure of Drayneflete Abbey. Better known, by far, is the delightful Drayneflete Carol, composed by an anonymous member of the community in the early fourteenth century, and now preserved in the British Museum (Drayneflete MSS. No. 6089–10–11) which was first sung on the occasion of a Yuletide visit to Drayneflete of the young Richard II. Although it has already been the subject of twenty-one talks in the Third Programme by Professor Harpsbaum, I print it here in full for the benefit of such readers who may still be unacquainted with this exquisite gem of Middle English prosody.

> Alle littel childer syng
> Prayses to our yonge Kyng
> Some syng sherpe and some syng flat
> Alma Mater Exeat.
>
> Alle engels in ye skie
> Maken loude melodie
> With sackbut, organ, pipe and drum
> Ad Terrorem Omnium.
>
> Ye povre beastes in ye stalle,
> Alack, they cannot syng at alle
> Ne cock ne henne of either sexe
> De Minimis Non Curat Lex.*

* The earliest known tune attached to this carol is generally attributed to Myrffyn ap Hwdda who was beaten to death with a lyre by a rival competitor at a late sixteenth-century Eisteddfod.

Although apart from the Prior's Lodging no traces of Drayneflete Priory exist today, two subsidiary establishments have happily survived. One is the Chapel of St Bodeswide standing on the quayside immediately behind the Town Hall, which was erected at the same time as the first stone bridge over the Drayne, and is now occupied by the County Food Office: the other is the ruined chapel of the Augustinians in the Littlehampton Memorial Park that received very rough treatment at the hands of 'the Gothicising improvers' responsible for laying out the park in the late eighteenth century, and has recently been incorporated into the People's Self-Service Refreshment Room and Cafeteria which was opened by the municipality last summer.

Of the secular remains of medieval Drayneflete virtually nothing remains. Gone is the exquisite old Custard Cross where the market price of custards (or costards) was regularly fixed by the master of the Custard Makers' Guild, and the memory of it survives only in a few rare seventeenth-century engravings; gone is the beautiful old Moot Hall, wantonly destroyed at the end of the seventeenth century to make way for a heavy and ill-proportioned building in the Renaissance style; gone the fine fourteenth-century hall of the Worshipful Company of Drumstretchers. Of the town walls, still standing in the eighteenth century, there remain a few traces of medieval masonry at the back of the cinema, miraculously laid bare by aerial bombardment and now carefully preserved; but of the wonderful old North Gate, represented in many old prints, not one stone remains upon another.

Of all the treasures of medieval Drayneflete, that of which the disappearance is to be, perhaps, most deeply regretted, is the old Fidget House, a miracle of half-timbering and carved newel-posts which stood, until well into the eighteenth century, up against the Prior's Lodging.

The remarkable family of Fidget, or ffigett, can boast a longer connection with the town than any other. The first Figet (or Fidget) of whom we have any record is Master Humfrey Figet whose effigy in brass lies in the south aisle of the Parish Church. The old theory that he was the son of a pawnbroker and 'contact man' for Prior Bloodwort had long since been disproved by the researches of the late Miss Dracula Parsley-ffigett who has conclusively shown that he came of a very ancient Welsh family of gentle birth. By the middle of the fifteenth century he was already

Master Humfrey Figet.
From a memorial brass
in the Parish Church.

the most prominent local citizen, being Master of the Custard Makers, twice Mayor and finally for a short time High Sheriff of the County. However, the great days of the family date from the time of the Dissolution of the Monasteries, when Master Humfrey's grandson Sir Jonas Fidget received a grant of Drayneflete Priory from the King, and must be left for further consideration in the next chapter.

Post-Reformation Drayneflete

The most important result of the reform of religion in Drayneflete was the disappearance of the Priory and the erection on its site (and with much of its materials) of the magnificent Tudor mansion of the Fidgets, happily still standing on the banks of the

Sir Jonas Fidget. From a portrait by an unknown artist now in the Art Gallery.

Drayne. A sincere friend of the reformed faith, except for a short period under Queen Mary, Sir Jonas Fidget played no small role in the glorious history of his times. Although he took no active part in the many voyages and explorations which rendered memorable the reign of the Virgin Queen, by financing, at a very reasonable rate of interest, numerous contemporary expeditions, he is entitled to a full share in the triumphs and glories of this great period of English History. With the cultural and artistic life of his time, his connection is less well-established. Tradition maintains that he is the original of the character Master Bloody, the miser, in the old play *Gaffer Gerkins Pryck* (attributed variously to Massinger, Beaumont, Fletcher, Greene and Kyd), and as a Justice of the Peace he sentenced a large number of contemporary poets and pamphleteers to have their ears cropped. Of his charitable and philanthropic activities, however, a concrete memorial remains in the shape of the Fidget Almhouses in the Station Road, and the school for poor scholars which originally stood hard by the bridge but which was transferred in the last century to the magnificent new building by Mr Waterhouse on Drayneflete Down. Dying at a very advanced age, 'from a surfeit of apricocks' according to the chronicler of the time, he was succeeded by his son, Sir Pompey Fidget.

Sir Pompey, the first baronet, had a distinguished military career in the Low Countries, where he trailed a pike in the Field

Sir Pompey Fidget;
the effigy on his tomb in the Fidget Chapel in the Parish Church.

Security Police, and was responsible for the apprehension of many dangerous characters in our ranks suspected of half-hearted acceptance of the Thirty-nine Articles or of communicating with the Jesuits. For his loyal services he was created a baronet and privileged to entertain his Sovereign at Fidget Priory, an honour which cost him almost as much as he had made out of the confiscations imposed on the traitors whom he had denounced. He was four times married, and lies beneath a handsome monument in the chapel which he added to the Parish Church. This effigy, which is a very fine example of contemporary sculpture, gains an added interest from the presence of his faithful hound, a feature which Mrs Esdaile regards as almost unique at this period and which makes the monument very popular with visitors, many of whom have signed their names in indelible pencil on the animal's hind quarters. Of his numerous offspring the most notable was his third son, Hezekiah, who left his native country during the last part of King James's reign, after a series of unfortunate financial reverses, for the New World, where he founded the town of Drayneflete, New Hampshire, and where his family is today worthily represented by Senator Wilbur P. Fidgett V.

Of the other Drayneflete worthies of the seventeenth century the most illustrious was probably that strange character, Dr Ezekiel Peppercorn, who is today best remembered for his discovery of the medicinal properties of the lesser bindweed, and his ingenious, though never-realised, project for a silent flush. In his own day his fame largely rested on his great work, *Hydrophilie or the Properties of the Fourth Element Explained, to which is appended an exact account of the marvellous great Privy in King Solomon's Temple.* He it was who was responsible for the notorious Drayneflete Water Riots in 1632. On this occasion a handsome new pump, the gift to the town of Sir Jeremy Fidget, who had long been anxious to provide his fellow citizens with a purer supply of drinking-water than that afforded by the River Drayne, was totally demolished by an angry mob inflamed by the eloquence of Dr Peppercorn who had preached two and a half hours on the text 'Are not Abana and Pharpar, rivers of Damascus, better than all the waters of Israel?' This remarkable character, who lived for fifty-six years in a house still standing, in Pump Court, finally died of a dropsy in his eightieth year and was buried in the church. In 1925 a memorial plaque was placed on No 2 Pump Court by the

The memorial to Dr Peppercorn in the chancel of the Parish Church.

Municipality and unveiled by the Chairman of the Metropolitan Water Board.

The seventeenth century was perhaps, anyhow in Drayneflete, richer in personalities than in monuments. The most noteworthy addition to the town during this period was the old Town Hall, a high-roofed classical structure, that was erected on the site of the Moot Hall in 1675. It was replaced by the present building in 1881, unregretted by all who knew it. The old Custard Cross had been wantonly pulled down some years earlier, on the specious plea that its style of ornament was Papist and that the shelter it afforded was conducive to immorality on wet Sunday afternoons.

Still stranger, perhaps, than their disregard of the claims of antiquity was the seventeenth-century public's unawareness of the true beauty of their own buildings; thus many of the fine old half-timbered houses erected during this period were covered by a flat wash of common plaster. Fortunately, more enlightened ideas prevail today and the Council has been at great pains to strip

Drayneflete: a general view of the town
in the mid-seventeenth century from a painting by the younger Truyp,
formerly in the Littlehampton collection, now in the Art Gallery.

Drayneflete at the end of the seventeenth century

DRUNK
ON YE
SABBATH

off this outer covering on such houses of that date as have now survived, thus revealing for the first time the full beauty of the glorious old oak beams.

The most remarkable of the existing buildings of this period is undoubtedly the King's Head Inn in the Market Place. It is known that an alehouse had stood on this site from very early times, but no part of the present structure, which has undergone numerous alterations in the intervening years, is older than the mid-seventeenth century. Of the distinguished travellers who have from time to time lain beneath its hospitable roof the name is legion. Although there is no mention of it in his diary, there is a firm tradition that Samuel Pepys frequently stopped here on his way to Dover and one of the bedrooms still bears his name. Likewise it has long been believed that it was at the King's Head that General Wolfe spent his last night in England and a copy of Gray's *Elegy* which he is said to have left behind is still preserved in the Smoking Room. (Albeit as it is the 1810 edition it is just possible that the general's own copy may perhaps have been purloined at some period and a substitution effected.)

Of considerable importance to the life and development of the town at this date was the arrival of the fourth Lord Littlehampton at Drayneflete Castle. This massive pile, which had been erected on the west bank of the Drayne shortly after the Conquest, had remained in the possession of the de Cowgumber family until the extinction of the male line on the execution of Sir Thomas de Cowgumber, his cousin Lord Cowgumber and his five brothers on Tower Hill in 1533. It then passed through the female line into the family of Lord Littlehampton who continued, however, to reside on their old Sussex estate at Courantsdair.

In 1672, however, the then Lord Littlehampton (the 'Wicked Lord') decided to leave his castle at Courantsdair and reside at Drayneflete, whence he could more easily reach his town house in Covent Garden. He at once set about improving his property and planned a mansion that was to rival in size Castle Howard or Seaton Delaval. Unfortunately funds ran out and only the central block was ever finished which must, adjacent to the still standing medieval ruins, have presented a very bizarre appearance. On his death in 1679 he was buried in the Parish Church where a magnificent marble monument, the work of an as yet unidentified sculptor, testifies to his virtues. The clustered banners and drums in the background recall the martial qualities of the deceased which were chiefly revealed during his tenure of the Office of Master of the Ordinance, a post he occupied during a short period of unbroken peace.

The sepulchral monument
of the fifth Viscount Littlehampton in the Parish Church.

The eighteenth century at Drayneflete was a time of rapid expansion during which the appearance of the town was considerably modified. Many of the splendid old timber houses were ruthlessly torn down and replaced by the square brick boxes which were the century's principal contribution to domestic architecture. Among the more elaborate buildings of this period should be noted the Corn Exchange in Market Street, half of which is still fortunately standing alongside Messrs Pixol's new show-rooms; the old Rectory, a fine red-brick mansion in the style of Sir Christopher Wren just behind the Church, which now houses the Drayneflete Museum and Art Gallery (*Open every day from ten till four. Entrance 6d. Special terms for schools.*) and an equestrian statue of William of Orange removed in 1897, to make way for the statue of Queen Victoria, to a new site behind the Town Hall.

The greatest of the many illustrious figures connected with Drayneflete during the period was undoubtedly Alexander, second Earl and eleventh Baron Littlehampton, the grandson of the 'Wicked Lord'. A man of wide culture and great sensibility, he devoted himself throughout a long life to the promotion of literature and the arts. The splendid collection of pictures that he formed has rendered his name familiar to all lovers of painting and his enlightened patronage supported numerous poets, architects and landscape-gardeners during their struggling years, and in some cases long after they had ceased to struggle. In his lifetime Drayneflete castle was twice completely rebuilt, first in the Palladian and then in the Gothic style. He it was who was responsible for 'Lord Littlehampton's Folly', an architectural curiosity expressly designed to display correct examples of all the five great schools of architecture. On ground level was a square pavilion from the façades of which projected classical porticos, in the Ionic, Doric, Corinthian and Tuscan orders respectively, adorned with numerous busts of Vitruvius, Palladio, Inigo Jones and other worthies. On this rested a Gothic octagon, pierced with traceried windows and sustained by flying buttresses, supporting a three-storied Chinese pagoda, that terminated in a cupola in the Hindoo taste. Under the whole structure was an Egyptian crypt. Completed in 1799, this curious freak remained intact until the night of its noble builder's death, when the oriental or uppermost sections were struck by lightning at the very hour when Lord Littlehampton was breathing his last. The Gothic octagon

The second Earl of Littlehampton ('Sensibility Littlehampton').
From a portrait by Pompeo Battoni, painted in Rome in 1769,
in the collection of the present Earl.

survived until 1923, when it was removed as being unsafe; while the classical pavilion on the ground floor remained comparatively intact until it was taken over by an AA battery as living-quarters for the ATS in 1941. Today all that remains is the Egyptian crypt which rendered yeoman service as an air-raid shelter for the inmates of the County Lunatic Asylum throughout the 'blitz'.

The best known of the numerous cultured figures who formed the Littlehampton circle was the poet Jeremy Tipple, but of him I shall speak at greater length when we come to consider the suburban development of the town.

Hardly less illustrious, however, was Dr Palinure, the celebrated Bishop of Horizon and the Isles. Born of humble Protestant stock on Lord Littlehampton's Irish estates at Spanielstown, his early promise soon attracted his Lordship's notice, and at his expense he was able to go first to Trinity College, Dublin, and later to Oxford. On leaving the University he became Personal Chaplain to his patron, who presented him with the living of Drayneflete at the first opportunity; to this were added in the course of time the livings of Belching-cum-Sowerby, Blicester, Great Danehampton, Toad-in-the-Wold, St Ursula-inside-the-Wardrobe and Stobdalkin in Co Meath. As the years passed and his fame grew he became Canon of Christ Church, Archdeacon of Bloomsbury, Dean of Spanielstown, Chaplain-out-of-the-Ordinary to his Majesty, and finally Bishop of Horizon and the Isles. Today these distinctions are largely forgotten but he lives in the memory of all as the author of that exquisite hymn (No 882, Hymns Ancient and Modern) which starts:

> How little, Lord, we need below
> As through this vale of tears we go.
> He doth all worldly goods despise,
> Who striveth for a heavenly prize.

Although few of his contemporaries enjoyed a greater reputation for learning, apart from the above-quoted hymn, his published works were confined to a volume of sermons and some translations of Ovid. The scantiness of literary remains should not blind us, however, to the real importance of the influence he exercised, supported by his wit and conversation, in contemporary thought and letters. In early life he was regarded as the principal inter-

Lord Littlehampton's Folly.

*The memorial to Dr Palinure
by a pupil of Flaxman in the Parish Church.*

preter of the ideas of the Encyclopaedists to the English public, a
role he successfully sustained although almost totally ignorant of
the French language, and by the more orthodox was looked on as a
convinced Latitudinarian, if not a Deist. Later, however, when the
French Revolution had made clear the terrible consequences of
loose thinking, he rallied strongly in support of Church and State,
and in his later years no one was more outspoken in his con-

demnation of all enthusiasm, and both Tractarians and Evangelicals had good cause to beware of the sharpness of his tongue. But despite the firmness of his convictions he was by no means an austere or unapproachable man: he kept the best table of all the bench of Bishops and left behind him in manuscript a collection of

*Sir Toby Fidget
by Kneller.
A portrait now
in the Art Gallery.*

128 different recipes for cooking trout. He was, moreover, the first clergyman ever to become a member of White's Club. He died full of years and honour in 1832 largely as a result of the exceptional exertion occasioned by his coming up to London when in a poor state of health, solely in order to deliver an unforgettable attack on the Reform Bill in the House of Lords. He died in his town house in Bloomsbury, but in accordance with his oft-expressed desire, he was buried at Drayneflete, where a fine marble monument to his memory, the work of a pupil of Flaxman, was erected by public subscription in the south aisle of the Parish Church.

Thanks to the establishment of Lord Littlehampton at Drayneflete Castle the prominence of the Fidgetts was a little reduced during this period, although their wealth increased and their social importance was considerably reinforced by the marriage of Sir Toby Fidgett, the grandson of Sir Pompey, with the eldest daughter of the 'Wicked Lord Littlehampton'. This lady,

'La Belle Fidgett' by Lely. A portrait now in the Art Gallery.

renowned for her beauty and high spirits, was known in Court circles, in which she passed much of her time, as 'La Belle Fidgett'. Her husband, a more placid type, devoted himself exclusively to the cultivation of tulips and the perfection of a gigantic water-clock that was still unfinished at his death. Their eldest son, Sir Hercules Fidgett, was a noted sportsman, whose

Sir Hercules Fidget by Stubbs. A painting now in the Art Gallery.

prowess in the hunting-field is still recalled in the Drayneflete country. His married life was not, alas, very happy; his wife, never being able to accustom herself to his lifelong habit of kennelling twenty or more hounds in the bedroom, finally ran off with the Master of an East Indiaman. However, these were but passing clouds temporarily obscuring the lustre of the house of Fidgett, and in the next chapter we shall see how its greatest triumphs were reserved for the nineteenth century.

Drayneflete early in the nineteenth century

Nineteenth-century Drayneflete and After

In Drayneflete, no less than elsewhere, the nineteenth century was a period of rapid expansion and long-needed improvement. Up to the accession of Queen Victoria the pace was slow, but after this happy event the rate of renovation and addition was much accelerated. This was, perhaps, less directly due to any personal influence that the young sovereign may have exercised on the course of local events than to the personality and far-sighted enterprise of that great philanthropist and worthy son of

Sir Jonas Fidgett. From a daguerreotype, formerly in the possession of Miss Amelia Parsley-ffidget.

Drayneflete, Sir Jonas Fidgett. Sir Jonas, who succeeded his grandfather Sir Hercules as fifth baronet while still a child, displayed on reaching years of discretion a strength of character and a public spirit that were to make a lasting impression on his native town. Marrying an heiress of great wealth, a Miss Parsley of Middlesex, and his own fortune having accumulated during his long minority to the dimensions that it had possessed before Sir Hercules had made the first of his many unsuccessful attempts to win the St Leger, he was in a position to devote himself whole-heartedly to public life. Entering Parliament in 1841 he represented his native town for over fifty years; as Justice of the Peace he gained for the Drayneflete Bench an enviable reputation for unflinching severity towards the malefactor. Three times Mayor, he was also chairman of the Drayneflete and Grand Junction Inland Navigation Co, of the Drayneflete and Southern Counties Railway Co (until its absorption by the SE and Chatham, on whose board he retained a seat), and the leading supporter of the principles of Free Trade in the Drayneflete district. A loyal Churchman of strong evangelical views, he was equally prominent in the religious and the philanthropic life, not only of the town, but of the nation. As President of the Society for the Maintenance of the Protestant Faith he was active in initiating the prosecution of many Tractarians and Puseyites; during his long tenure of the Chairmanship of the Society for the Evangelisation of the Hottentots he was directly responsible for the translation of the works of Isaac Watts into Bantu, Swahili, Tamil, Tanaggu and Amharic; as founder and principal benefactor of the Fidgett Home for the Daughters of Mentally Afflicted Gentlefolk, of the Fidgett Home of Rest for Indigent School-Masters and of the Society for the Prohibition of Games of Chance, he gained a reputation that extended far beyond the confines of his native town.

In the town itself, apart from the noble statue in the Market Place, Sir Jonas is today principally commemorated by the splendid Town Hall, the work of Mr (afterwards Sir) Giles Clerestory, RA, of which the foundation-stone was laid by HRH the Prince of Wales in 1881, and the entire cost of which the generous baronet defrayed with a characteristic munificence. On the events of a day that was to prove ever memorable in the annals of the town a lively account is preserved in the files of the *Drayneflete Advertiser:*

HRH The Prince of Wales laying the foundation-stone of the new Town Hall in 1881.
From a contemporary photograph now in the Mayor's Parlour.

1. HRH The Prince of Wales. 2. The Third Earl of Littlehampton. 3. Sir Jonas Fidgett, Bt. 4. Lady Fidgett. 5. Master Jasper Fidgett. 6. Colonel Wicker. 7. Canon Hassock. 8. Archdeacon Stavely-Locker. 9. His Worship the Mayor. 10. The Recorder. 11. Giles Clerestory, Esq, RA. 12. Miss Wicker. 13. Captain Hydrant.

Many a Drayneflete heart rejoiced this morning on looking out of the window and perceiving blue skies half hidden by a slight haze which augured well for the prospects of this auspicious day. By 10.45 a large crowd was already waiting when the Committee of Welcome arrived in a flashing cavalcade at the Railway Station. First came Lord Littlehampton, a dignified martial figure in his plumed hat and full-dress uniform of Lord Lieutenant, riding alone in an open landau behind a spanking team of the celebrated Littlehampton greys. Close behind followed His Worship the Mayor with the Town Clerk, Alderman Catchpenny and our worthy beadle, in an elegant equipage which did much credit to Messrs Jollyboys Livery Stables. Outside the station was drawn up a Guard of Honour formed of the No 1 Company of the Drayneflete Volunteers under the command of Major Wicker, the martial bearing and smart appearance of which was generally commended by their fellow townsmen, and the Town band under the able direction of Mr Register who for this occasion had exchanged the more familiar surplice of organist for the gold brandenburgs of Band-master. After the Lord Lieutenant had inspected the guard and been received by our popular station-master, Mr Coupling, the whole party proceeded onto the No 2 down platform which had been covered by a noble red carpet (kindly provided by Messrs Pelmets, House Furnishings and Upholsterers, No 3 High Street) and enlivened by large tubs of hydrangeas, the splendid appearance of which did much credit to Messrs Mould and Puddle, Florists, No 7 Station Road.

At 11.3 precisely the Royal train drew alongside and after a slight confusion occasioned by a sudden change in the position of the Royal Saloon, His Royal Highness, looking bronzed and fit, alighted and was received by Lord Littlehampton, who introduced His Worship the Mayor, who thereupon read an address of welcome in the elegant phraseology and beautiful expression of which we fancy we detected the hand of our respected schoolmaster, Mr Grigson. This done, His Royal Highness graciously consented to accept a bouquet from the hands of little Miss Coupling and with his usual affability insisted on shaking hands with her father, our worthy station-master.

As soon as the Royal Party appeared at the station entrance the band burst into a lively rendering of *God Save the Prince of Wales*, while cheer upon cheer broke from a thousand loyal throats. Having inspected the Guard of Honour, His Royal Highness entered the Lord Lieutenant's landau and, preceded by the Band, the procession moved off to the heartening strains of the Grand March from *Norma* through richly decorated streets to the Market Square.

On arrival at the site of the new Town Hall His Royal Highness was received by a Committee of Welcome consisting of Sir Jonas and Lady Fidgett, Canon Hassock, the Chief Constable and Captain Hydrant, chief of our gallant Fire Brigade whose stalwart men formed the Guard of Honour. After His Royal Highness had shaken hands with the members of the Committee and Sir Jonas had presented to him Master Jasper Fidgett, Mr Clerestory the architect, and the foreman of the works, he received a silver trowel from the hands of the last and unhesitatingly advanced to the foundation-stone, tapping it with unerring precision in the exact centre, saying as he did so in a strong clear voice, 'I declare this stone well and truly laid'. Thereupon Canon Hassock offered up a short but beautiful prayer of his own composition and the choir accompanied by the band lifted up their voices in *Rock of Ages* in the singing of which all the company joined. It was particularly noted that His Royal Highness although not, perhaps, familiar with all the words, followed the singing with a deep and reverent attention, occasionally humming a bar or so in a light but pleasing baritone.

House Party at Ffidget Priory.
Left to Right. *Standing:* Sir Ephraim Kirsch, Countess Droshky, HE
the Bavarian Ambassador, Sir Jasper Parsley-Ffidgett, Bt, Lord
Spanielstown, Col Hon Odo Currander, and 'Bimbo'.

1907.

Seated: HSH The Grandduchess Olga of Luneburg-Wolfenbüttel, Miss Shelmerdine Parsley-Ffidgett, Hon Lady Parsley-Ffidgett, the Dowager Countess of Littlehampton.

Sir Jasper Parsley-Ffidget, Bt.
From the painting by Sargent,
now in the Art Gallery.

The Town Hall, however, was not the only building in Drayneflete to benefit from the liberality of Sir Jonas. He it was who was the principal promoter of, and the largest subscriber to, the fund for the restoration of the parish church carried out in the 'seventies, under the supervision of Sir Gilbert Scott. The moulded plaster ceiling of eighteenth-century workmanship which had for so long concealed the beautiful open-timber roof was removed, as were also many of the fittings such as pulpit and altar-rails of the same date. In their place were substituted a beautiful new rood screen in cast bronze relieved with enamel-work, a fine stone pulpit (designed in free imitation of the baptistery of Pisa) and an exquisite reredos in carved soapstone, the work of a talented Munich designer. At the same time many of the windows, which had hitherto been plain white, were enriched with stained glass commemorating various families of the town.

On the death of Sir Jonas in 1898 he was succeeded by his only son, the youngest of a family of eleven, Jasper. Although in a way no less a public figure than his father, the fields in which the seventh baronet triumphed were rather different. Educated at Eton and Christ Church, Oxford, he inherited many of the sporting instincts of his great-grandfather, Sir Hercules, though in his case an early and persistent interest in horse-flesh was later overshadowed by enthusiasms more in keeping with the age. One of the earliest of motoring enthusiasts, his De Dion Bouton was the first automobile ever to be seen in Drayneflete and he was for many years a regular competitor in the Gordon Bennett Balloon Race. On leaving Oxford he served for a short period in the Foot Guards and subsequently as honorary attaché in Vienna; only relinquishing the latter appointment on his marriage to Lady Consuelo Currander, the only daughter of the fifth Earl of Littlehampton. On the outbreak of the 1914 war he rejoined his regiment and served with distinction on the staff of GHQ Cairo for the duration of the conflict. Such architectural changes as came about in Drayneflete in his lifetime were largely the result of commercial and municipal enterprise, and apart from adding a new wing, together with a garage, to Ffidget Priory, he was responsible for little building. Nevertheless, in the little that he did do he was careful to preserve the old-world character of his historic home and both the garage and the new wing were gabled, tile-hung and elaborately half-timbered. Lady Consuelo Parsley-

ventieth-century Drayneflete

Shelmerdine, only child of Sir Jasper and Lady Parsley-Ffidget. From a painting by Modligliani, now in a private collection.

Ffidgett was a woman of great taste and keen interest in the arts and devoted all the later years of her life to making a carpet for the Great Hall in exquisite *petit-point* to a specially commissioned design by Sir Frank Brangwyn.

On the death of Sir Jasper Ffidgett in the 'twenties, at a comparatively early age (his health had long been precarious and he had latterly spent much time in private nursing homes), he left an only child, a daughter, Miss Shelmerdine Parsley-Ffidgett. Of astounding beauty, her début in London Society immediately after the 1914 war was long remembered, and her natural gaiety and high spirits made her a very popular member of the 'younger set'. She married, first her cousin, the eighth Lord Littlehampton (marriage dissolved 1923), second, Sophocle ('Soffie'), Duc de Vichy-Celestins (marriage dissolved 1928), third, Prince Vladimir Doppelchinsky (marriage dissolved 1931), fourth, Hiram P. Hatzenbacker II of Long Island, NY. Her tragic death in 1935 as the result of an accident at a midnight bathing-party on the Eden Roc came as a great shock to all who knew her, the last of a family which for over five hundred years had played so prominent a part in the history of Drayneflete.

Of the many changes which have overtaken the centre of the town in the period between the wars the illustrations will speak more convincingly than any words: while the considerable suburban development on the other side of the river is of so interesting and extensive a nature that it deserves a chapter to itself.

Top: A. Cultural Monument scheduled under National Trust ('Poet's Corner'). B. Gasometer. C. Clover-leaf crossing and bridge. D. Communal Housing Block. E. Lunatic Asylum and Littlehampton Memorial Park. F. Cultural Monument scheduled under National Trust. G. Municipal Offices including Community Centre, Psychiatric Clinic, Crèche and Helicopter Landing-strip on the roof. H. Housing Estate for higher-income brackets. I. Communal Sports Centre, Yacht

The Drayneflete of tomorrow

Club and Football Ground. J. Floating Concert Hall for audience of 2,500 and full symphony orchestra. K. Power Station.

Bottom: A. Communal Housing Blocks. B. High-level Pedestrian road-bridge. C. Cultural Monument scheduled under National Trust. D. People's Restaurant, Swimming Club, Bathing Pool, Cinema and Amenities Centre. E. Under-ground Station.

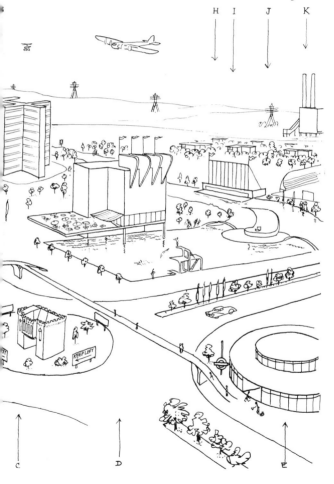

Poet's Corner

At the beginning of the nineteenth century the main road to the coast was practically unflanked by buildings after it crossed the river by the old bridge and a ten-minutes walk from the Market

Jeremy Tipple, Esq, poet. From a portrait by Knapton, now in the Art Gallery.

Place in this direction was sufficient to take the traveller into virgin country. A little more than a mile from the bridge there was a cross-roads at which stood a single humble inn opposite the recently completed walls of Lord Littlehampton's great park. The second Earl, 'Sensibility Littlehampton' as he was known, at the time of the second rebuilding of Drayneflete Castle conceived the kindly idea of building a small Gothic Lodge at this corner of his estate for his friend and protégé, the poet Jeremy Tipple. It was the long residence of this celebrated bard in this villa which first gained for the cross-roads the appellation 'Poet's Corner', and it was here that he wrote his immortal *The Contemplative Shepherd*, a poem of some fifteen thousand lines of which we can, alas, only quote a small selection. The passage chosen is of particular topographical interest as the landscape described is today almost entirely covered by the municipal sewage farm.

> Th'enamelled meadows that can scarce contain
> The gentle windings of the limpid Drayne
> Full oft have seen me, wandering at dawn
> As birds awaken and the startled fawn
> Leaps from her mossy bed with easy grace
> On catching sight of my indulgent face.
> Deep in some crystal pool th'enamoured trout
> Frolics and wantons up a lichened spout
> By which the stream, in many a sparkling rill,
> Is made by art to turn a water-mill.
> At last the sluggard Phoebus quits his bed
> And bares the glory of his fiery head;
> Now all the world assumes an aspect new
> And Nature blushes 'neath the mantling dew.
> E'en yonder mossy walls and em'rald sward
> The home of Littlehampton's puissant lord,
> The ancient fastness of a warrior race
> Regards these marches with a kindlier face. . . .

1800

1830

By 1820 both the poet and his patron were dead. Owing to the slump at the end of the Napoleonic Wars, coupled with a bad run of luck at Crockfords, the nephew and successor of the second Earl ('Sensibility Littlehampton' had never married) had been forced to sell land for development and a row of gentlemen's villas to the design of Mr Papworth had been erected alongside Poet's Corner, while a bailiff's cottage in the Rustic style was erected on the further side of the inn some years later. The Gothic Villa itself was now in the possession of Miss Amelia de Vere, the only child of the poet's married sister, Sophonisba, who had long kept house for her brother. Along with the house Miss Amelia had inherited much of her uncle's poetic gift, although at first this was only revealed to a small circle of intimate friends. After, however, the anonymous publication of her *Lines on the Late Massacre at Chios*, which sounded like a tocsin throughout Liberal Europe, her fame was assured. It is not, alas, possible, nor indeed is it probably necessary, to quote this celebrated work in full, but the two opening verses will serve to demonstrate both the fearless realism of the gentle poetess and her exceptional command of local colour, a command the more extraordinary in that she never, save for a brief visit to Turnbridge Wells, travelled more than ten miles from Drayneflete in all her life.

> O hark to the groans of the wounded and dying,
> Of the mother who casts a last lingering look
> At her infant aloft, understandably crying,
> Impaled on the spear of a Bashi Bazook
>
> O see where the vultures are patiently wheeling
> As the scimitars flash and the yataghans thud
> O innocent victims, vainly appealing
> To dreaded Janissaries lusting for blood.

However although Miss de Vere may have never, save in imagination, set eyes on distant parts she was afforded many a complete change of scene on her own doorstep in the course of an extraordinarily long life. The first transformation was due to the coming of the railway. In order to save a considerable diversion and the expense of building a bridge over the Drayne, the main line kept to the south bank of the river and the station was located

Miss Amelia de Vere.
From a miniature by Sir George Richmond,
formerly in the possession of Bill Tipple, Esq.

1860

rather more than a mile from the centre of the town, close by Poet's Corner cross-roads, and the permanent way was carried over the coast road by viaduct. This development coincided with another of Lord Littlehampton's bad runs of luck at Baden-Baden (furthermore the noble Lord had suffered grievously by the repeal of the Corn Laws) and he took the opportunity of selling off all his property to the north of the railway.

The opening of the railway and the subsequent increase in importance of this hitherto unimportant suburb led to further rapid development. In 1855 the successful termination of the Crimean War was commemorated by the erection of a memorial fountain and the Duke of York public-house acquired a new façade. At the same time the increase in the congregation of the ancient church of Drayneflete Parva, half a mile up the hill, thanks to the recent completion of Gotha Terrace and other residential streets on what had previously been virgin fields, encouraged the churchwardens to add a spire to the somewhat squat tower.

At the time of Miss de Vere's death in 1890 the developments described above had been carried a stage further and the whole district was beginning to lose something of its hitherto exclusively residential character. The Duke of York was completely rebuilt in 1885, and four years later the Drayneflete Gas Company's Works were established alongside the railway to the south. The villas adjacent to Poet's Corner were gradually turned into shops, and the new streets which came into being at this time were largely built for the convenience of a lower grade of society.

The third Earl of Littlehampton, dying at an advanced age in 1883, largely due to the shock sustained after a peculiarly bad run of luck at Homburg, was succeeded by his grandson, a man of simple tastes who divided his time between the family seat at Courantsdair and his Irish home at Spanielstown. In the Jubilee year he sold Drayneflete Castle for a lunatic asylum and presented the grounds to the Municipality as a public park.

On the death of Miss de Vere, Poet's Corner passed to her nephew, Mr Casimir De Vere-Tipple, in whom the poetic gift, so constant in this remarkable family, burnt, if not with renewed vigour, certainly with a 'hard gem-like flame'. His contributions appeared regularly in *The Yellow Book*, and were published in a slim volume by the Bodley Head under the title *Samphire and Sardonyx*. Unfortunately he did not long enjoy his property as he

The third Earl of Littlehampton
in the uniform of Colonel-in-Chief of the Drayneflete Yeomanry.
From an engraving after a portrait by Sir Francis Grant, PRA.

1890

was forced, for private reasons, to live abroad from 1895 onwards and thenceforth resided on Capri in a charming villa where his great social gifts and exquisite hospitality will still be remembered by many visitors.

Casimir de Vere-Tipple, Esq.
From a drawing by Jacques Émile Blanche.
Reproduced by kind permission of the Trustees of Tate Gallery.

After the departure of Mr de Vere-Tipple the Poet's Corner was let on a long lease to a firm of monumental masons. A further great change in the appearance of the neighbourhood occurred when, shortly before the 1914 war, Messrs Pinks, the drapers, entirely rebuilt their premises and a confectioner's acquired the space between them and the Poet's Corner. The secluded quiet of this once shady nook was further interrupted by the substitution of trams for horsebuses at the turn of the century, and the subsequent increase in traffic due to the coming of the internal combustion engine.

However, the poetic tradition of the locality was not even yet extinct. On his death in 1929 Mr de Vere-Tipple left this valuable site to his favourite nephew, then at Oxford, Guillaume de Vere-Tipple, who had already made a name for himself by the publication of *Feux d'artifice* (Duckworth 1927), a collection of verse astonishing in its maturity, from which we quote a single poem, *Aeneas on the Saxophone.*

> . . . Delenda est Carthago!
> (ses bains de mer, ses plâges fleuries,
> And Dido on her lilo á sa proie attachée)
>
> And shall we stroll along the front
> Chatting of this and that and listening to the band?
>
> The plumed and tufted sea responds
> Obliquely to the trombone's call
> The lecherous seaweed's phallic fronds
> Gently postulate the Fall.
>
> Between the pebble and the beach rises the doubt,
> . . . Delenda
> Between the seaside and the sea the summons,
> . . . est
> Between the *wagon* and the *lit* the implication,
> . . . Carthago.

1925

Bill Tipple.
From a still from the film 'Whither Democracy',
reproduced by kind permission of the C of I.

In the years between the wars the whole character of the district was still further altered. In 1930 Messrs Watlin acquired the Duke of York, which was at once rebuilt in a contemporary style which, although it at first struck those accustomed to the brassy vulgarity of the old 'pub' as strangely austere, was soon generally agreed to be both socially and aesthetically an immense improvement. Two years later another even more daring example of 'the

Modern Movement'; as it had come to be known, arose in the shape of the Odium Cinema. While some of the more old-fashioned residents might find fault with the functional directness of this great building, nothing but praise could be accorded to the modified Georgian style in which the new Council flats across the road were built at much the same date.

The coming of a new age, of which the buildings round Poet's Corner were a portent, found a reflection in the poet's verse. Guillaume de Vere-Tipple was socially conscious to a remarkable degree and had long entertained doubts as to the security of capitalist society, doubts which received striking confirmation when International Nickel, in which he had inherited a large holding, slumped to $11\frac{1}{2}$. Making a clean break with the past, his next volume of poetry, *the liftshaft* (Faber and Faber 1937) appeared above the signature Bill Tipple, and, as may be seen from the poem quoted below, this reorientation is reflected in the contents:

crackup in barcelona

among the bleached skeletons of the olive-trees
stirs a bitter wind
and maxi my friend from the mariahilfer strasse
importunately questions a steely sky
his eyes are two holes made by a dirty finger
in the damp blotting paper of his face
the muscular tissues stretched tautly across the scaffolding of bone
are no longer responsive to the factory siren
and never again will the glandular secretions react
to the ragtime promptings of the palais-de-danse
and I am left balanced on capricorn
the knife-edge tropic between anxiety and regret
while the racing editions are sold at the gates of football grounds
and maxi lies on a bare catalan hillside
knocked off the tram by a fascist conductor
who misinterpreted a casual glance.

The late war dealt hardly with Poet's Corner. Fortunately the house itself is still standing, but the confectioner's next door was totally demolished and extensive damage was caused to much of the surrounding property.

After the end of the conflict, in a misguided effort to relieve the considerable local housing shortage, an estate of pre-frabricated dwelling-houses was erected by the Borough Council in what had been erstwhile the shady groves and green retreats of the Little-hampton Memorial Park.

Today Poet's Corner is up for sale: its owner, Bill Tipple, who on the outbreak of war had been a conscientious objector, but who, on hearing the news of the invasion of Russia, experienced a complete change of heart and immediately joined the Drayneflete section of the National Fire Service, is absent for long periods abroad in his capacity of organising secretary of the World Congress of International Poets in Defence of Peace. The long Littlehampton connection with the town is now a thing of the past; the great race of Ffidgets is extinct. But their spirit lives on and their successors on the Borough Council are determined that the Drayneflete tradition shall at all costs be maintained. But, whatever the future may hold in store, let the visitor reflect as he goes round the Museum, as he inspects the magnificent collection of Ffidget portraits in the Art Gallery (bequeathed to the town in 1948 by the late Miss Dracula Parsley-ffigett), as he wanders in the old-world Market Place, as he paces the banks of the 'limpid Drayne', let him reflect on the men and women who through the ages have all played their part in making Drayneflete what it is today, and see to it that we, their heirs, shall prove ourselves worthy of so goodly a heritage.

The
Littlehampton
Bequest

DRAYNFLETE ABBEY

FOR VIOLET AND TONY

Contents

TITLE-PAGE ILLUSTRATION: Drayneflete Abbey, from a 17th-century woodcut.

Foreword

Few collections representative of the whole history of English portraiture can rival that of the Littlehamptons of Drayneflete. Van Dyck and Lely, Reynolds and Gainsborough, Romney and Lawrence, Burne-Jones and Millais, Sargent and Hockney are but a few of the artists whose work adds lustre to a collection notable above all for its richness in the likenesses of those who have shaped this island's history. The Littlehampton Bequest therefore rightly constitutes, in one magnificent gesture, the most significant addition to the National Portrait Gallery's holdings since the last war. Thanks to the enthusiastic persistence of the Countess of Littlehampton in her negotiations with Her Majesty's Government (and much to the relief of the Editor of the letters page of *The Times*) the Littlehampton Collection has passed intact to the nation. It is of course greatly to be lamented that space will not as yet permit even a temporary display of these historic treasures. In the meantime, however, a careful programme of cleaning and conservation is being carried out under the expert direction of Dr Ernest Swaboff, whose restoration of the *Drayneflete Madonna*, now in the National Gallery, already stands as a monument to his ingenuity in recovering what had for long acted as a section of the chancel floor in the Chapel at Drayneflete. At the same time research into the history of the family and the detailed documentation of each portrait is being undertaken by Miss Provenance of our curatorial staff.

The Drayneflete Collection is an historic one long referred to in the annals of art in this country. Indeed the earliest reference to the collection occurs in the Notebooks of that pioneer of the history of the arts in England, the antiquary George Vertue. On February 26th 1720 Vertue visited the collection and described it as follows: 'Drayneflete – seat of the Earl of Littlehampton – in the gallery. Cleopatra by Cranach, Sir Nicholas de Littlehampton by

Gerrat and several other olde pictures on bord – in the hall – Lord Drayneflete on horseback by Van Dyck. fine.' Thereafter some reference to the Drayneflete portraits figures in every description of the great houses of this country from the peregrinations of Pennant and Dr Syntax to the charming account of the house in *The Beauties of England and Wales* (1815) and Dr Waagen's critical appraisal in the 1854 edition of his *The Treasures of Great Britain and Ireland.* Not long after the earliest scholarly catalogue of the collection was compiled by Lady Ethel Littlehampton. This was printed in a limited edition of one hundred copies with the finest portraits reproduced in sepia photogravure. With this the serious academic study of the Littlehampton Collection may be said to begin. My predecessor, Sir Lionel Cust, soon after contributed an article to *The Burlington Magazine* reconstructing the *œuvre* of an early English portrait-painter he called the 'Drayneflete Master', since unfortunately proved to be the work of no less than three separate painters, French, Italian and Dutch. Thenceforward items in the collections have been the subject of lively interchange in the world of learning.

It remains for me to say how indebted the Trustees are to Mr Osbert Lancaster for recording for us the results of his researches into the Littlehampton family and their portraits.

ROY STRONG

National Portrait Gallery

Introduction

When it was suggested to me by Dr Strong that I should provide some biographical notes for this sumptuous catalogue of a magnificent bequest, I readily and delightedly agreed. Although not a professional historian, a longstanding friendship with the family and a close familiarity with the house and its contents encouraged me to believe that I could overcome the disadvantages imposed by an amateur status. In so far as I may be thought to have done so, it is largely due to the limitless encouragement, unbounded enthusiasm and extraordinary range of information of the present Countess. Indeed had I not had Lady Littlehampton constantly by my side, while my task might have been concluded far sooner, it would have been infinitely less enjoyable. To her and the Earl I owe a debt of gratitude which the present volume can only inadequately discharge.

To those of my readers who may chance to be acquainted with an earlier work, dealing with the history and antiquities of Drayneflete,* some apology, I feel, is due for certain discrepancies which they may detect between the two texts. Much additional research has been carried out in the Littlehampton Archives in the last twenty years and, moreover, I must confess that in the former work I relied a little too confidently on the authority of a distinguished local historian, the late Miss Dracula Parsley-ffigett, herself a member of an ancient and distinguished country family, who was certainly enthusiastic but neither professionally trained nor invariably impartial. Thus her claim that her niece Consuelo was ever married to, let alone divorced from, the present Earl is quite without foundation. The cousins were certainly good friends and there were at one time rumours of an engagement but no banns were ever called. Less important but

* *Drayneflete Revealed* (John Murray, 1949).

perhaps more aggravating is her constant carelessness about dates and generations, thus the 3rd Earl is regularly referred to as the 2nd and the 4th as the 5th, etc. Equally exasperating is her phonetic spelling of the family name 'Courantsdair' (pronounced Currander) – an error which arose, presumably, from dictation. Far less forgivable, however, is the quite unjustified assertation that the 6th Earl sold Drayneflete for a lunatic asylum and public park in 1887. The facts are as follows. Spending all his time on his Scottish estates and never coming South the 6th Earl threw open the park to the public on Sundays and holidays when the family were not in residence. Some years later after the break-up of his first marriage, the 7th Earl leased the North Wing to a Home of Rest for the Mentally Underprivileged of Gentle Birth of which his sister, the Lady Ethel, remained the enthusiastic patron until, in 1946, it came under the administration of the Ministry of Health.

Readers should, therefore, bear in mind that invaluable as the former volume may be for those interested in the local history of Drayneflete or the genealogy of the Parsley-ffigetts, as a chronological account of the Earldom of Littlehampton it is less than reliable. The author hereby apologizes for his errors of twenty years past and trusts that the present biographical notes will have served finally to put the record straight.

O.L.

The Littlehampton Bequest

When the 3rd and last Earl of Littlehampton, of the first creation, lost his head on Tower Hill, having unfortunately backed the wrong Rose, the sole remaining representative of this illustrious family was his infant daughter, Agnes. As all her father's vast estates were forfeit to the Crown, his treasure dispersed and the great Keep of Courantsdair dismantled, her lot was miserable indeed. The poor waif was finally taken by her devoted nurse to a small priory at Sloppingham in Norfolk, of which a distant cousin on her mother's side was Prioress, where it seemed likely that, undowered as she was, she would end her days. However, she grew into a lively and attractive child and at High Mass one Lammastide she caught the eye of a rich merchant from Lynn, who had some farms in the neighbourhood, and by Candlemas they were man and wife.

Nicholas Wouldbegood was one of the most successful and important of 15th-century tycoons, with a fine house in Lynn from the watch tower of which he could keep an eye on his merchant-men, anchored in the Ouse, and with counting-houses in London and Bruges. With the accession of Edward IV, whose fondness for the company of successful businessmen, and their wives, was as marked as that of his seventh namesake four hundred years later, his influence was much increased and in 1480 he was granted a Royal Letters Patent to adopt the name and arms of de Courantsdair.

Perhaps as a result of the penury she had known as a child, it is recorded that Dame Agnes soon developed a head for business no whit inferior to her husband's and used regularly to accompany him on his travels both to London, where she was soon welcome in Court Circles, and to Bruges, where it seems likely that this exquisite likeness, the right panel of a triptych of which the centrepiece is now in the Metropolitan, was painted.

About the identity of the artist there has been much dispute; Friedlander at first assigned it to one of the Van Eycks, but Dvŏrăk detected in the painting of the background the unmistakable hand of Dirk Bouts. At the moment it would seem wise to accept the current attribution to the Master of the Foolish Virgins, so called after his masterpiece formerly in a church in Hertogenbosch, long since vanished, by whom no other work whatever is known to exist. Of the opposite panel, which presumably exhibited a portrait of Master Wouldbegood, no trace, alas, has ever been found.

DAME AGNES DE COURANTSDAIR
Master of the Foolish Virgins [?]

The exact date of Wouldbegood-Courantsdair's death has not been established but his widow, who was many years his junior, was still flourishing in the early years of Henry VIII's reign. Their eldest son, Benjamin, who inherited both his father's acumen and his mother's political adroitness, soon attracted the notice of the young sovereign. To his wide knowledge of foreign parts and command of languages was added, after the fall of Wolsey, a zealous enthusiasm for the Reformed Faith. With these advantages his career at Court, in days when there existed no professional diplomatic service, advanced rapidly, and was suitably rewarded. In 1548 he was made a Clerk to the Privy and was able to acquire, for a very reasonable sum, all the lands and buildings of Drayneflete Abbey, and the following year he was knighted.

Of his first wife we know little. She was the daughter of an Alderman of the City of London and a Past Master of the Drumstretchers' Company and did not, reportedly, come to him empty-handed. Their marriage although apparently happy was comparatively brief as she died of the plague after presenting him with two daughters and a son, born in successive years.

In difficult times Sir Benjamin's sound sense and unswerving devotion to the monarch's interests enabled him to avoid every pitfall. In King Edward's reign he enjoyed the position of an elder statesman and received the Priory of Sloppingham, the scene of his parents' romance, together with eleven farms and a water-mill as a testimony of his sovereign's affection. With the accession of Queen Mary, his business interests caused him to spend much time abroad and it seems likely that he died while on a visit to his second wife's relations in the Palatinate.

He left a very considerable fortune to his sons but did not neglect the poor and needy for whom he provided on a generous scale. Today his benevolence is still remembered annually on the first Thursday after Epiphany with the distribution in the churchyard of St Ursula-inside-the-Wardrobe, of 'Old Ben's Bounty', as it is commonly called, a blood-pudding, a bundle of faggots and two groats apiece, to twelve indigent but sober old men residing in the parish.

BENJAMIN DE COURANTSDAIR
School of Holbein

Many would claim that this exquisite masterpiece is the gem of the whole Bequest; none could dispute that it possesses the most romantic history.

At a time when King Henry VIII was hoping to establish closer relations with the Protestant Princes of Germany, Sir Benjamin found himself on a secret mission to the Court of the Elector Maurice of Saxony. One day this affable ruler took the English-man on a visit to the studio of his friend and protégé, Lucas Cranach. Here the visitor was immediately struck dumb by the beauty of a panel of Cleopatra by the banks of the Nile about to drain the fatal draught in which she had previously dissolved a pearl, which he at once acquired and took back to his lodgings. The more he gazed on his purchase the more determined he became to make the acquaintance of the fair original. Luckily this did not prove difficult as Cleopatra, under the name Gertrud von der Leberkranz, was well known in Court Circles. She was the daughter of a celebrated Captain of *landsknecht*, Gottfried von der Leberkranz, and a 'liberated' nun (whether her birth took place before or after the liberation is not recorded), and received her visitor with her habitual courtesy and charm. Albeit she was now a few years older than she appeared in the painting, her admirer's expectations were abundantly fulfilled and he straightway offered her his hand which was immediately accepted. (This is the only recorded instance of Sir Benjamin ever having acted on impulse.) A few days later, after a brief ceremony in the Court Chapel, the King's emissary returned to his native country with his painting and his bride. Of the latter's subsequent history we know little. She presented her husband with a son soon after the homecoming and both as a wife and widow occupied a much respected position in the City's Lutheran community. She died in 1575 and was buried in the Dutch Church at Austin Friars where her beautiful tomb survived the Great Fire, only to fall victim to the ferocity of her fellow countrymen in 1941.

For many years this wonderful picture was completely lost sight of, until the present Countess located it in the servants' hall, to which it had been relegated by the 5th Countess, a woman of strong principles, after she had commissioned her friend, Mr Frith, RA, to provide her predecessor with a thick flannel night-dress, now happily removed.

'CLEOPATRA'
Lucas Cranach the Elder

[180]

While inheriting to the full his father's business enthusiasm, Sir Nicholas's ambitions became, with time, increasingly dynastic. Pulling down what remained of Drayneflete Abbey he built himself a splendid many-windowed manor-house in the contemporary style on the site. He married, early in Queen Elizabeth's reign, the younger daughter of the 9th Baron Venison, generally referred to in Court Circles as 'the Haunch'. Her family was known to be impoverished, and suspected of being recusant, but for the bridegroom her lack of dowry and, it must ungallantly be added, looks, were more than compensated for by the distinction and number of her quarterings, and the marriage was a singularly happy one.

However, while establishing himself ever more firmly in the ranks of the landed gentry Sir Nicholas did not neglect his commercial interests which tended, however, to become more exclusively financial in character as time went on. Despite the fact that in Gheeraerts's portrait his finger is apparently resting on the Caribbean, there is no evidence that he himself ever went further west than Hampton Court. Nevertheless his was an important and glorious role in the great expansionist movement of this Golden Age; few syndicates of which he was a member ever produced an unfavourable balance sheet and on his death, at the turn of the century, he left his elder son, Christopher, vast estates and an immense fortune in bullion.

On the magnificent Courantsdair tomb, formerly in St Ursula-inside-the-Wardrobe,* the splendid effigies of himself and wife are accompanied by the kneeling figures of their nine children only three of whom reached riper years, and surmounted by innumerable blazons. Unfortunately the artist responsible for Lady de Courantsdair's portrait here reproduced remains unknown, but his work is distinguished from that of the majority of his contemporaries by a certain charming naturalism which finds its happiest expression in the treatment of the infant in arms.

* Transferred to the Chapel of Drayneflete Abbey after the demolition of St Ursula's in 1968.

SIR NICHOLAS DE
COURANTSDAIR,
Bt.
Marcus Gheeraerts

LADY
DE COURANTSDAIR
Artist unknown

Of Sir Benjamin's son by his second marriage we unfortunately know little. He would seem not to have had much in common with his half-brother, spending more time at Court than in the counting-house where he soon gained a reputation as a skilled poetaster and a dexterous performer in the pavane. As a young man he spent some years in the household of the Earl of Southampton and there are those who maintain, but Dr Rowse is not among them, that he was the original Dark Lady of the Sonnets.

He was known, at least on one occasion, to have trailed a pike in the Low Countries when there were those among his companions who loudly proclaimed that in his case 'trailed' was the operative word.

With the accession of James I his social success markedly increased and no masque was regarded as worth the watching in which he did not have a prominent role, but with the onset of middle age he rapidly put on weight and his sovereign's anxiety to have him always about his person became less acute. At the same time his half-brother's reluctance to pay the debts which his personal extravagance incurred became more marked, and soon the Court revels knew him no more. He ended his days in almost total obscurity, living on the charity of his nephew. He never married.

AUBREY DE COURANTSDAIR
Nicholas Hilliard

Among the many carefree young gallants at the Court of King Charles I few cut so dashing a figure as Christopher de Courantsdair. High-spirited, handsome and enormously wealthy, he was equally popular with both sexes and his devotion to the House of Stuart was absolute. When the war broke out he immediately placed himself and his fortune at the disposition of his sovereign and none among the Cavaliers surpassed him in gallantry, although it must be admitted that few displayed such tactical incompetence.

With the final defeat of the Royal cause he accompanied the Heir Apparent into exile, loyally remaining at his side until the Restoration. It is pleasant to record that his devotion did not go unrewarded; not only were his estates restored to him, but on his marriage to an old friend of the King he was created Viscount Drayneflete and made Master of the Ordnance, and he continued high in the Royal favour until the very end of the reign. It was, perhaps, the jealousy such marked favour aroused which earned him the title of 'the Wicked Lord', for it is hard to see that he exceeded in iniquity the majority of his contemporaries. While it is just possible that the tale of his seduction of the eleven-year-old daughter of the Bishop of Barnstaple in her father's vestry may have some foundation in fact, there would seem little to justify the frequent charges of sodomy. On the only occasion that he appeared before a magistrate, on a charge of indecent exposure in the Mall – 'flashing his Littlehampton' as the Court wits put it – the principal witness was discovered to be a notorious Anabaptist and the case was dismissed. He died in 1675 and was buried under a plain slab, later replaced by the 1st Earl who, at the time of his rebuilding of the Abbey, commissioned the mortuary statue from the celebrated Rysbrack in 1729 for the Littlehampton chapel in Drayneflete Church.

THE VISCOUNT DRAYNEFLETE
Van Dyck

When Viscount Drayneflete went into exile with his sovereign he was accompanied by his younger brother Guy. A studious and, compared to his brother, unglamorous youth, he soon abandoned the Royal entourage in the Low Countries and made his way to Rome, where he not only reverted to the faith of his mother's family, but took Orders. Great was the rejoicing in Vatican circles at the return to the fold of so prominent a lost sheep, and he was soon comfortably installed in the household of Cardinal Azzolino where, it is said, he played an important part in the conversion of Queen Christina.

Amiable and hospitable, his apartments in the Palazzo Condotti became in time a place of pilgrimage for his countrymen passing through Italy, among them John Evelyn, who viewed his extremely comfortable way of life, and in particular 'a little sloe-eyed serving wench', with Protestant disapproval. While conscientious in fulfilling all his ecclesiastical duties he did not abandon those sporting diversions characteristic of an English gentleman and was reckoned the best shot in the Curia; nor did he neglect to cultivate scholarly pursuits, publishing a large folio volume, *De Gustibus Romanorum*, in which he gives no less than thirty-two different recipes for stuffing a partridge.

When in 1769 the 3rd Earl of Littlehampton was in Rome on the Grand Tour he had the curiosity to visit his great-great-uncle's lodgings which he found to be carefully preserved, in the condition in which he left them at the time of his death, by a withered crone of immense age (could this have been John Evelyn's 'sloe-eyed serving wench'?) from whom, with some difficulty, he managed to acquire this splendid bust.

MONSIGNOR DE COURANTSDAIR
Bernini [from a contemporary engraving]

Louise, the young wife of the elderly Baron de Stellenbosch who did so much to render life tolerable for King Charles II during his exile, was said by general report to have come from an armigerous Walloon family residing in Antwerp, but there were those who declared her to be the natural daughter of the Cardinal-Archbishop of Utrecht. Whatever her origins all were agreed on her beauty and her sympathetic nature. She first met the exiled monarch under her husband's roof and a rewarding and comparatively longstanding relationship soon developed. When the King came into his own again she accompanied him in London, the Baron having tactfully died a month or two earlier, but it is sad to have to relate that their delightful intimacy did not long survive the sea-change. Yet, despite new involvements, the monarch remained ever mindful of all her kindness and saw to it that she was firmly established in a state suitable to her rank, and upon her marriage to his old friend, Sir Christopher de Courantsdair, the bridegroom was immediately raised to the peerage and the bride received not only a number of very good livings but also a monopoly on the import of Dutch gin.

At Court where she immediately secured, and long retained, a prominent position, she commanded universal admiration and her charms were celebrated in the verses of Rochester and the paintings of Lely. 'To the playhouse', writes Pepys, 'where I was mightily pleased to find myself in company with my lady Drayneflete.' Towards the end of her life she became notably pious and developed an extraordinary enthusiasm for sermons, the longer the better, although it was generally agreed that her pew in the Chapel Royal was always well supplied with that commodity of which she enjoyed the monopoly.

THE VISCOUNTESS DRAYNEFLETE
IN THE CHARACTER OF ARTEMIS
Sir Peter Lely

Augustus de Courantsdair succeeded his father, the 1st Viscount Drayneflete, while still a child. Coming of a family devoted to the Stuarts and with an uncle at the Vatican, it might have been thought that he had a great future at Court, but his natural sagacity rendered him mistrustful of King James's chances, and in fact few of the nobility gave so enthusiastic a welcome to Dutch William. His foresight was soon rewarded and after the Battle of the Boyne, at which he arrived, a little late, at the head of his own company of horse, he was made the 1st Earl of Littlehampton of the second creation.

The new Earl's first action was to embark on the rebuilding of Drayneflete in a style more suited to his rank. For the house itself he called in Mr Hawksmoor, who made short work of the old Elizabethan mansion, from which he retained only the Long Gallery. For the gardens he solicited the advice of the great Le Nôtre himself in Paris and for the decoration of the Great Saloon he relied on the talents of Sir James Thornhill. In the year that this great enterprise was finally completed he married Vanessa, only child and heiress of Sir Solomon Bunbury, Bt, a former Lord Mayor of London, possessed of vast estates in the West Indies.

'Il Magnifico', as he was commonly called by his contemporaries, in reference to his lavish personal expenditure coupled with a certain haughtiness of manner, while playing no very public part on the political stage, exercised a powerful influence behind the scenes. In the last years of Queen Anne's reign no man did more to counter the intrigues of Harley and Bolingbroke and to secure the Hanoverian succession. The importance of the role he played was fully realised by the new sovereign's advisers and in the Coronation Honours List he received, at long last, the Garter. In 1742 at the age of seventy-three he suffered a choleric seizure in his coach, provoked, so it is said, by the insolence of a toll-keeper to whom he was forced to take a horse-whip, and died before reaching home. He was survived by his wife and four children.

THE 1ST EARL OF LITTLEHAMPTON, KG
Sir James Thornhill

The 1st Earl's marriage to the only daughter of the immensely wealthy Sir Solomon Bunbury, Bt, a Lord Mayor of London who, it was said, owned half the plantations in the West Indies, might well be described as 'à la mode', but thanks to the strength of character displayed by both parties the outcome was far removed from the dismal débâcle in which Hogarth's characters were involved. The bride, whose mother had been a Miss ffossil of Norfolk, inherited not only the beauty which had made that lady the Queen of the Swaffham Assembly Rooms but much of the energy which her grandfather had so successfully displayed in the management of his estates. Of the grandeur of her husband's position she was, from the first, fully appreciative and by her wit and by her social talents did much to enhance it. In Laroon's delightful canvas she is shown in mourning for her husband, who had died the previous year, and accompanied by her two daughters, Letitia and Euphemia with, in the background, her devoted page Hasdrubal, who had been born on her father's estate in Jamaica. This engaging blackamoor was held in the highest esteem by the whole family and his mistress took a particular pleasure in his company and insisted on his being always about her person. The Lady Letitia never married but, on the tragic death of her elder brother, devoted herself to the upbringing of her little nephew the 3rd Earl. The Lady Euphemia, on the other hand, whose irrepressible gaiety and strangely exotic beauty attracted innumerable suitors, survived three husbands: the 3rd Marquess of Tumbledown, who died in his seventy-eighth year, shortly after their marriage; Prince Ludwig of Kilmansegg-Lauterbach who fell at the Battle of Minden; and lastly Lord Jonathan Firturse who was killed in the hunting-field. The Countess herself lived on to welcome her grandson's first bride to Drayneflete and passed peacefully away at the faro table in 1772.

VANESSA, COUNTESS OF LITTLEHAMPTON
AND HER DAUGHTERS
Marcellus Laroon

William, the 'Magnifico's' only son, cuts, perhaps inevitably, a rather dim figure alongside his illustrious parent. Not naturally gifted, what talents he possessed were not furthered by his education which, apart from a year or two at Winchester, took place largely in the stables and the servants' hall. However, it would be unwise unreservedly to accept the assertion made by Lord Hervey in his memoirs, that he was totally illiterate; abundant evidence exists in the Drayneflete muniment-room showing that he could write his own name very neatly. He remained a bachelor until after his succession to the title on his father's death, when he married a Miss Grosgrain who came, so it was claimed, from a very old Huguenot family. According to Hervey, who is clearly in this case a prejudiced source, he had first 'known' his bride when she was a fourteen-year-old still-room maid.

Although never commanding the immense respect in which his father had universally been held, the 2nd Earl was generally admitted to have been a superb horseman, a very capable Master of Hounds, and was very highly thought of in local cock-fighting circles. Not politically active, his only speech in the House of Lords, which has not alas survived, was described by a fellow peer as being 'incoherent but forthright'; he was a staunch upholder of the Hanoverian Succession and the Established Church, and his numerous pocket boroughs were always at the disposal of the Whigs. Happy in the place, if not the manner, of his death he was killed, at a comparatively early age, in a duel on Newmarket Heath by a certain Colonel Clapstock whose casual remarks on the parentage of his sister, the Lady Euphemia, he had much resented and whom he had, rather unwisely, challenged.

In Seymour's splendid canvas he is shown astride his celebrated stallion 'Hudibras' accompanied by his favourite bitch 'Clytie' from whom the whole of the existing Drayneflete pack directly descend.

THE 2ND EARL OF LITTLEHAMPTON
James Seymour

The younger of the two sons of the 1st Earl, who was born but a year before his father's death, was intended for a military career, but two events combined to change his vocation after he had served for only eighteen months in HM Foot Guards. First there seemed every likelihood that his regiment would be sent overseas; second, the incumbent of Coltsfoot Canonicorum, one of the best-endowed livings in his brother's gift, died unexpectedly. Accordingly he resigned his commission, went up to Pembroke College, Oxford, and took Holy Orders.

It might well be thought that a youth passed in the carefree atmosphere of St James's would have proved an unpromising preparation for a clerical career, but such, it seems, was far from being the case. Joined to his brother's passion for rural sports was a fine literary taste and an enquiring mind and the young vicar was very soon contentedly settled in his remote parsonage. Within a year of his arrival he had excavated a Druidic dolmen in his kitchen garden of which in due course he published an illustrated account. This was followed first by *A Description of the Antiquities in the Hundred of Ballsoken* and some years later by *Hengist and Horsa*, a two thousand line poem in heroic couplets which achieved considerable contemporary success although little read today. Of the author Dr Johnson is recorded as saying 'Sir, a man who can make so prodigious a brick with such a scant quantity of straw has a just claim to the amazed consideration of his fellows'.

In addition to his published works he kept a careful diary in which, under the date 4/IX/'78, occurs the following passage: 'Today my likeness by Mr Stubbs came from the framemaker. I am well satisfied altho' methinks the cheeks are a little too full. Hannah, with the perversity of her sex, was enraptured by the painting of the house to the exclusion of all else. This evening had Squire Coltsfoot and a few friends to supper. All loud in their praise of Mr Stubbs' genius. A good turbot, a dish of sweetbreads, a side of veal, two ducks, a saddle of lamb, sidedishes, and syllabubs.'

This estimable gentleman died in 1792 sincerely mourned by all his humble flock and by his many friends in the world of letters. He was survived by his widow – he had married his housekeeper in middle age – and an only son, Hengist, whose twin brother, Horsa, had died in infancy.

THE REVEREND THE HON DR LANCELOT DE COURANTSDAIR
George Stubbs

From his earliest youth – much to the distress of his parents – Hengist Courantsdair had been tainted with Enthusiasm. He frequented the company of Methodists and hedge-preachers and even in his schooldays was much given to Pentecostal outbursts. Some attributed this strange flaw in his character to his mother's side – it was rumoured that her grandfather had been, when young, a Fifth Monarchy man – others to the Huguenot influence of his aunt. Unfortunately this intemperate zeal was not confined to matters of religion, and he was soon notorious in the district for the loud expression of social and political views which could only be described as Jacobinical.

It was, therefore, not regarded as entirely a matter for regret when at the age of seventeen he ran away to America, the cause of whose newly liberated citizens he had always enthusiastically promoted. For many years nothing was heard, but by the end of the first decade of the new century, he was recorded as being established, having Anglicised his name, in Ipswich, Massachusetts, as a timber merchant. That his business was modestly successful is proved both by the existence of the old Coriander House on Argyla Road (now carefully preserved by the Ipswich Historical Society), and his marriage to a Hackenshaw of Newburyport.

With increasing prosperity his religious enthusiasm would seem to have taken second place to his commercial interests, although he was still regularly Moved by the Spirit to denounce the iniquities he saw flourishing around him. It is not recorded that he ever revisited the old country, but that all family ties were not completely broken is suggested by the presence in the Bequest of this charming example of the Primitive Art of the post-Colonial period.

His union was blessed by seventeen children of whom the most remarkable was Jethro, the third son. Obeying the contemporary injunction to 'go West' this young man founded the town of Littlehampton, Ohio, where he established a foundry, which supplied large quantities of cannon to the North during the war between the States (and if rumour is correct, quite a few to the South). From him the present head of the American branch of the family, Senator Jethro P. Coriander III, First President of The No Guaranty Trust of Philadelphia, of Consolidated Deterrents, of Napalm Products Inc, etc, etc, is directly descended.

HENGIST AND ABIGAIL CORIANDER
Artist unknown

Born in 1749, the 3rd Earl succeeded his father at the age of twelve. His mother being rather slow-witted and a foreigner to boot, his early upbringing was largely entrusted to his aunt, Letitia, his father's unmarried sister. A bright and promising lad, he went to Merton College, Oxford, and thence on the Grand Tour, accompanied by one of the younger Fellows, the Reverend Doctor Fontwater. This proved to be the great formative experience of his life, and the enthusiasm for antiquity and the arts he then acquired was never abated. During his absence, and for months after his return, a constant stream of packing-cases was delivered at Drayneflete containing Roman marbles and Greek vases, canvases by Salvator Rosa and Raphael Mengs, medieval manuscripts and Renaissance bronzes. As soon as these were installed he at once set about improving his surroundings, and called in Capability Brown to remodel the Park on the most approved modern principles. The lines of Le Nôtre's great avenues were ruthlessly twisted and broken; the formal canals were transformed into a chain of picturesque lakes; on every hillock well-sited elm clumps were planted, concealing grottoes and temples, and no vista lacked an eye-catching Folly. Immediately after his first marriage he decided the time had come to bring the house itself into conformity with its new setting. He therefore called in Mr Wyatt, who made short work of Hawksmoor's pilasters and rustications and, by the introduction of pointed windows, crockets and castellations, restored to the ancient Abbey that ecclesiastical air which His Lordship's ancestors had been at such pains to banish. The changes were, however, largely external; inside, the Long Gallery, the only part of Sir Nicholas's original house to have survived, was carefully preserved and Thornhill's Great Saloon and the rest of the State Apartments were fortunately left untouched. However, a Gothic chapel was added to the south of the West Wing on what were thought to be the remains of the original abbey church but which recent research has shown to have been the site of the Abbot's wash-house.

In Reynolds's noble portrait the Earl is shown holding the plan of the excavations at Pozzuoli, carried out by the Dilettanti Society, of which he was a prominent member, and indicating the exact spot on which he himself found the celebrated bust of Scipio Africanus now in the British Museum.

THE 3RD EARL OF LITTLEHAMPTON
Sir Joshua Reynolds, PRA

In 1775 the 3rd Earl married Louisa, fourth daughter of the 2nd and last Duke of Buxton, a prominent member of the Whig Establishment. Her childhood had been sadly clouded by her father's disappointment at the Duchess's failure to produce an heir, which he did little to conceal from his wife or his offspring. This, acting on a nature prone to melancholy, had induced in her a permanent lowness of spirits which might well, given a husband less ebullient than the Earl, have rendered her marriage disastrous. But although they could never have been described as kindred spirits, she did her best to take an interest in her husband's artistic pursuits while he, concealing his irritation at her lifelong inability to distinguish between Correggio and Caravaggio, encouraged her efforts, never, alas, wholly successful, to master the harpsichord.

Her death, a year or two after the birth of their only child, Agatha, in 1782 filled him with genuine distress only partially assuaged by the erection of a magnificent mausoleum in the Saracenic style to his own designs.

It is said that on certain nights of the full moon a gentle rustle of silks is still heard passing down the Long Gallery, the door to the Green Drawing-Room opens and shuts of its own accord, and a moment or two later the midnight silence is softly broken by the strains of a particularly lugubrious aria from Handel's *Semele* rather tentatively played on one finger.

THE COUNTESS OF LITTLEHAMPTON
Thomas Gainsborough, RA

The younger brother of the 3rd Earl did not share, in any marked degree, the intellectual and cultural tastes for which his senior was justly renowned. Although he accompanied his brother on the Grand Tour, Venus rather than Minerva was always for him the favoured goddess, provoking his tutor to remark that 'if this devotion should continue unabated it is greatly to be feared 'twill only lead to a lifelong dependence on *MERCURY*'. A commission was therefore procured for him in one of His Majesty's ships of the line.

In the course of a long and distinguished career in the Senior Service his most notable exploit ws undoubtedly the capture of Fort Shittipore, a strongly defended island in the Bay of Bengal, an achievement which was splendidly recorded in an enormous painting by John Singleton Copley, of which, alas, it has been possible to illustrate only a detail. Although the artist was not himself present at the battle, he spared no pains, as was his custom, to inform himself of every relevant detail before setting brush to canvas. Unfortunately, the long account of the action written by Major Flintlock, commanding the Marines (which is confirmed, incidentally, by the private diaries of the Reverend Doctor Fontwater who was serving as Chaplain to the expedition) was not at that time readily available. According to this, the attack was launched at dawn, the fort finally falling at 11 in the forenoon, and the Admiral did not himself come ashore until shortly before sundown.

Having, as a result of this victory, acquired a very considerable sum in prize-money and the ribbon of the Bath (which by a curious oversight on the part of the artist he is here shown wearing some eighteen months before the award was in fact made) he retired from the Service, married the Hon Lavinia Ballcock, the eldest daughter of Admiral the Viscount Bulwark, and purchased a fine estate in the neighbourhood of Sidmouth, rebuilding the house, which he renamed Shittipore, in the Hindu style to the designs of Sir William Chambers. He died at a very advanced age leaving seventeen children, none born in wedlock.

THE CAPTURE OF FORT SHITTIPORE [*a detail*]
John Singleton Copley

Joseph Grumble came of what is euphemistically described as good yeoman stock. As a lad his appearance was engaging and his intelligence well above the average and he soon attracted the attention of the local parson who not only saw to it that he received a rather better education than other boys of his rank in life but, when adolescence was past, obtained for him a clerkship in the East India Company. The good old man's generosity was abundantly rewarded, for Joseph was never a man to neglect his opportunities and within a very short time he was well established as an Assistant Inspector of Taxes in the State of Buggeribad. Fulfilling his official duties with competence and regularity he nevertheless had sufficient time on his hands to go into jute and, to a lesser extent, teak and spices, and had by the age of thirty-five amassed a very considerable fortune which increased annually. By the time that William Hickey came to Madras he was installed in one of the finest houses of the town and maintained a state second only to that of the Governor himself.

He was married three times, but the rigours of the climate, by which he himself appeared to be quite unaffected, proved too great and all his wives predeceased him, as indeed did all his children save Louisa, his youngest daughter by his third wife. In Zoffany's fine canvas, painted in 1786, shortly before the old man's final retirement, he is shown on the veranda of his great house surrounded by his servants and accompanied by his little daughter. In little more than a year after the picture was completed both were back in England comfortably installed in the splendid estate of Drayneflete Magna, only a stone's throw from the Abbey, which he had at once acquired.

It is interesting to record that the little girl's faithful *ayah*, shown on the extreme right in the picture, accompanied her young mistress back to England where she was soon converted to the true faith, became a prominent member of the Countess of Huntingdon's Connection, and married an eminent shipschandler in Bristol.

JOSEPH GRUMBLE ESQ
J. Zoffany, RA

When Joseph Grumble on retirement established himself as a country gentleman it seems likely that his choice of residence was guided by the 3rd Earl of Littlehampton's younger brother, with whom he had established a firm friendship when the Admiral was on the East India station. It is beyond doubt that this old association was responsible for the friendly relationship which rapidly developed between the neighbouring landowners. At this time the 3rd Earl was beginning to find widowerhood irksome and it is hardly surprising that the Nabob's little daughter, a remarkably early developer, should have attracted his friendly notice. Moreover he could hardly have been unaware, as the bills for all his architectural improvements steadily mounted, of the immense fortune she was likely to inherit. It was, therefore, no surprise to their intimates when, on her fifteenth birthday, Miss Grumble, with her father's blessing, and a large settlement, became Countess of Littlehampton. To the world at large, however, this love-match quickly became a topic for eager, and not invariably kindly, speculation. 'Has His Lordship told you, madam', writes Horace Walpole to the Countess Ossory, 'of Lord Littlehampton's affecting romance. . .? Juliet it appears is not much more than five-and-thirty years junior to Romeo but I suppose the latter judged the young lady's jointure far outweighed the exertion of scaling a balcony. The thought of what he will do with all those lakhs of rupees is beyond my conjuring. The last time I was in that part of the country his park was so full of whimsical additions that you could not see the wood for the pagodas. The Nabob is said to be mightily pleased. Whether Iphigenia considers a coronet sufficient recompense for her sacrifice is only to be guessed at.'

Horace Walpole need not have worried; the young bride is reported to have manifested the greatest enthusiasm for her new role, and it was not long before her wit, beauty and vivacity became the talk of the town. Within two years the happiness of her indulgent spouse was crowned by the birth of two boys. As soon as she had fully recovered the Earl, taking advantage of a temporary lull in European hostilities, set off with a numerous train to familiarize the young Countess with the wonders of his beloved Rome. It was on this occasion that he commissioned the celebrated Canova to immortalize her beauty in marble.

THE COUNTESS OF LITTLEHAMPTON
Canova

Within less than a year of the death of the Earl, his Countess, who was still a young woman, married the Hon Sysonby Flannel, the second son of the 3rd Viscount Cheddar, an Ensign in HM Foot Guards. Their union was idyllic but brief, the gallant bridegroom falling at Corunna, whereupon, after a due period of mourning, his widow was joined in wedlock to Sir Tresham Manifest, Bt, HM Minister Plenipotentiary in Stockholm, whom she duly accompanied to the Congress of Vienna where he was number two in the British delegation. In 1815, on the very eve of the final session, the world learnt with astonishment that Her Ladyship had bolted with General Prince Goloshkin, an ADC to the Tsar, leaving her husband with their eighteen-month-old son. The scandal was immense and the guilty pair went into exile in the Ottoman Empire. After a time, however, the Tsar's wrath abated and the Prince, now legally married, was permitted to take up an attachment at the Russian Mission to the Sublime Porte.

It was in the course of an official visit to the Holy Land that the Prince's party were overwhelmed by a band of marauding Arabs in the neighbourhood of Damascus. The Prince barely escaped with his life and his wife was carried off to adorn the harem of the leader. For some years nothing more was heard of the Princess, and then travellers' tales of a beautiful European lady, the principal wife of an immensely rich Alawit Sheikh, who was presiding over a miniature court in a handsome castle in the mountains behind Latakia, began to filter back. Soon a regular flow of European pilgrims to the Holy Land turned up at her residence; all reported that, although no longer young, the former Countess had retained all her remembered beauty and fascination. She soon became known as the 'Ninon de l'Enclos du Levant' and so powerless was age to wither her charms that it is reported that, when in her seventies, she successfully seduced Mr Holman Hunt on the shores of the Dead Sea, thus delaying the completion of *The Scapegoat* by several weeks. The exact date of her death is unrecorded but she was buried beneath an elegant *turbeh* on the heights overlooking the B'qaa which remains to this day a popular place of pilgrimage for devout Alawits.

'LE CABINET D'AMOUR'

THE HON
SYSONBY
FLANNEL
*Artist
unknown*

PRINCE GOLOSHIKIN
Daffinger

THE COUNTESS
IN
EASTERN DRESS
J. F. Lewis

SIR TRESHAM MANIFEST, Bt
After Lawrence

SHEIKH ABD'L BOUBA
Qajar School

The elder son of the 3rd Earl was, from all accounts, cursed with a strangely unsettled character; inheriting his mother's passionate nature (although, not, alas, her looks) without her shrewdness, his father's extravagant bent was not, in him, redeemed by those artistic tastes which had earned the 3rd Earl the soubriquet of 'Sensibility'. He was renowned for his wit, of which Captain Gronow has in his memoirs recorded a characteristic example. At a party at Carlton House, meeting with a Duchess celebrated for her massive charms, he seized an arum lily from a near-by vase and plunging it into her corsage remarked, 'Allow me, madam. A lily for your valley!' – a pleasantry which earned him exclusion from Almack's for a whole year.

Even in the Regent's circle his capacity for hard liquors was conspicuous and the same diarist informs us that he was accustomed to consume brandy and orange curaçao 'in quantities fearful to behold'. His successes with the fair sex were legendary, of which that which excited the greatest envy among his contemporaries was his seduction of the fifteen-year-old Carlotta Cannelloni, whose affections he retained for a number of years. This remarkable girl, in whose company he is shown in the accompanying plate, early in life displayed a soprano voice of quite extraordinary power and range which her protector arranged to be trained by the most admired masters of the day, with such success that a few years after this likeness was taken she enjoyed a memorable success at Drury Lane creating the role of Elfrida in *La Muette de Portici*, and continued to enrapture vast audiences in all the opera-houses of Europe for more than thirty years.

His end was tragic; on leaving a splendid banquet in the Pavilion celebrating the Regent's birthday he insisted, against all advice, on driving himself back to his lodgings. The night was foggy and he had the misfortune to drive himself and his curricle off the end of the chain pier. His horse had the good luck – or the sagacity – to swim ashore, but the 4th Earl made his last public appearance a few days later in a fisherman's net off Bexhill.

Note. The accompanying hand-coloured engraving is attributed in the Littlehampton Catalogue to Gillray, but I can find no reference to it in the authoritative and exhaustive volumes which Mr Draper Hill of Boston has devoted to the master. Moreover, the Brighton Pavilion was only completed in its present form in 1811, a date by which Gillray, who died in 1815, had almost ceased to practise his art.

'BEAU LITTLEHAMPTON'
From a contemporary engraving by Gillray [?]

Joseph, who succeeded to the Earldom on the tragic death of his elder brother, was a man of very different stamp. Serious-minded and public-spirited, he spoke frequently, and at length, in the Upper House. However, despite his loyalty to the Whigs and his support for the Reform Bill, which involved the disappearance of the two-member constituency of Coltsfoot, the most profitable of his pocket boroughs, public office always eluded him; by how narrow a margin is revealed in the following letter from Creevey: 'Dined with the Seftons, also there Wickedshifts, Sydney Smith, Lambton and "Pomposo" Littlehampton. The last refused to speak to Wickedshifts whom he regards as being responsible for his being out of office. Apparently he was confidently expecting the Admiralty and was furious at being offered Woods and Forests, without a seat in the Cabinet. After Wickedshifts had left he explained to me and Sefton how well suited he was to the former post as his uncle had been an admiral! Was there ever?!'

After this setback the Earl devoted himself largely to his arboretum and local affairs and as a JP and later Lord-Lieutenant (in the uniform of which high office he was painted by Winterhalter) earned for himself the unstinted admiration of all his neighbours. He still appeared in the Upper House from time to time, when the Whigs could always rely on his vote, and usually a long and cogently argued speech justifying his support for whatever government measure was under discussion. This unswerving devotion to Whig principles did not pass unnoticed and Lord Melbourne, during his second administration, made him a Privy Councillor, in which capacity he attended the historic meeting on the accession of Queen Victoria. He died of an apoplectic fit while reviewing the Volunteers on Drayneflete Common in 1865 and was succeeded by his only son who at once inherited the Earldom, but had to wait for some years yet for his mother's Barony.

Today the 5th Earl is chiefly remembered for the *Cupressus patrescens*, or Littlehamptonia, as it is popularly called, which was first raised in Drayneflete Park.

THE 5TH EARL OF LITTLEHAMPTON
F. X. Winterhalter

The 5th countess was born Dorothea MacStruth, the only child of Sir Alistair MacStruth, Bt, and Lady Lochwhistle of Lochwhistle, a Baroness in her own right. From both parents she inherited large estates in Scotland and from her mother the Barony.

Brought up as a strict Presbyterian, she displayed, even as a young woman, a remarkable firmness of character which did not escape the notice of Mr Creevey: 'Went to Holland House where I found a large party including "Pomposo" and his bride. The latter a formidable, fine-looking young person – another Lieven – if you can imagine *that* lady with a Scots accent and a Presbyterian conscience! Old Madagascar in one of her worst moods, but the Hieland Lassie gave as good as she got. "Pomposo" his usual self. When I said in my last letter that Lord Tullamore was the greatest bore in London I was wrong!'

The Countess's character did not soften with the years. While remaining a staunch Presbyterian north of the Border, in London she gave her full support to the Evangelical wing of the Established Church, was a regular patroness of revivalist meetings in Exeter Hall and a leading figure in the Temperance Movement. Her dominance of her husband was, in later life, absolute. As previously recorded she clothed and removed to the servants' hall Cranach's splendid *Cleopatra* and she it was who banished into outer darkness Canova's superb statue of her mother-in-law, whose very name could not be mentioned in her hearing. Only when she ordered all his French brandy to be poured down the sink is it recorded that the Earl made his single, but ineffectual, protest. With her daughter-in-law, whose marriage she had done so much to promote, her relations were never easy; mistrustful of her artistic activities she was scandalized by her Tractarian leanings, and after a monumental row on the vexed subject of the Eastward Position the two ladies never again exchanged a word.

THE COUNTESS OF LITTLEHAMPTON
F. X. Winterhalter

As the years went on the 5th Earl became increasingly worried by the predicament of his half-sister, his father's child by his first wife. This lady lacked not only those superficial charms likely to attract suitors of her own rank but was wholly dependent on the generosity of her half-brother. It was, therefore, with a cheerful and uncharacteristic disregard for social distinctions that he gave his consent to her marriage to the Reverend Aloysius Fontwater, a penniless curate and youngest of the eleven children of old Dr Fontwater, the 3rd Earl's tutor. By great good fortune the living of Colstfoot Canonicorum had been left, ever since the death of the Reverend the Hon Lancelot, in charge of a curate who was now replaced by the Reverend Fontwater. A year or two later, through the influence of an uncle on his mother's side, who was the Senior Warden of the Worshipful Company of Drumstretchers, he was presented with the important and well-endowed living of St Ursula-inside-the-Wardrobe. Very shortly afterwards he became a Prebendary of St Pauls.

A staunch middle-of-the-road man, his contempt for the Evangelicals was only exceeded by his detestation of the Puseyites; an eloquent preacher with powerful Whig connections, it was clear that the Reverend Aloysius had a great future ahead of him, and his appointment to the See of Barnstaple, caused no surprise. Soon after his induction, however, the new Bishop became involved in one of the great ecclesiological controversies of the period. His cathedral, in a poor state of repair, was due to be rebuilt and the work had been entrusted to Mr Butterfield, a notorious Tractarian. The Bishop immediately cancelled the contract only to discover that he had acted *ultra vires* as the decision rested with the Dean and Chapter who insisted firmly on their rights. However, they had sadly underestimated their man. Before he knew where he was the unfortunate Dean found himself up before the Consistory Court to answer charges of simony, rejection of the doctrine of Baptismal Regeneration and misappropriation of the Easter Offering. The Archbishop was forced to intervene and finally the Bishop withdrew the charges and the Chapter agreed to replace Mr Butterfield by Sir Gilbert Scott. Dr Fontwater was the last bishop regularly to wear a wig in the House of Lords.

THE RIGHT REVEREND
BISHOP FONTWATER
From an engraving by J. Phillips

THE LADY AGATHA
FONTWATER
Artist unknown

Alistair, the son and heir of 'Pomposo', was described by the more indulgent of his relatives as a 'child of nature'. Never happier than when in the company of dumb animals, as a lad he spent far more hours in the kennels than in the schoolroom. Born into a humbler rank of society he would have made an admirable vet and, indeed, among his Highland neighbours he was regarded as the leading authority on softpad.

His parents, however, felt that this specialised talent would not of itself equip him to manage his estates, and had soon regretfully to recognise that he possessed no other. This was the more serious as the 5th Earl was himself financially embarrassed. His father's building activities had made serious inroads on the Littlehampton fortune, his mother's vast Grumble inheritance she had taken with her on remarriage, and he was for long burdened by the necessity of discharging his late brother's enormous debts.

It was not surprising, therefore, that when Sir Ebenezer Horse-ferry acquired the estate adjoining Lochwhistle the Countess should have cast a speculative eye on her neighbour's daughters. Great was her joy when it became apparent that Alistair regarded the fair Louisa with an affectionate interest almost as great as that aroused by his Labrador bitch.

The resultant marriage was not unhappy. True the husband spent most of the year on his Scottish estates while the wife always passed the whole season in London; nevertheless they enjoyed sufficient time in each other's company to produce eight children. In his wife's artistic activities the Earl took no interest, although he did consent to sit to Sir Edwin Landseer, the only artist for whom he ever expressed any admiration, for his portrait, while the Countess who had inherited her father's taste along with his collection, as well as her mother's musical talents, shunned the moors and devoted herself to stalking Pre-Raphaelites in Cheyne Walk.

In 1889 the Earl was so unfortunate as to be knocked out by a falling ptarmigan of exceptional size, an accident from which he never fully recovered, dying the following year. He was survived by his widow who passed peacefully away, while reading Dante on the terrace of her lovely villa above Fiesole, some few years later.

THE 6TH EARL OF LITTLEHAMPTON
Sir Edwin Landseer, RA

In the latter half of the 18th century there flourished, in the little town of Muddlesborough in the North Riding, a young blacksmith named Jonas Horseferry. Largely self-taught, but exceptionally shrewd, he recognised sooner than most the nature of the great change that was then taking place in rural industry, enlarged his forge, set up a smelting-yard and by the turn of the century had become one of the most successful ironmasters in the county. He married, in the year of Trafalgar, the daughter of a local Methodist minister who duly presented him with a son and heir, Ebenezer.

Thanks to his mother Ebenezer received a rather better education than his father whose partner he soon became. Under his direction the family business expanded fourfold and when in 1837 he married a daughter of the manse, he brought his bride home not to the modest farmhouse on the hills above the town, where his father had recently died, but to a splendid mansion in the Jacobethan style which the genius of Mr Salvin had caused to arise on the site. With the coming of the railways his already large fortune vastly increased and encouraged by his wife, a woman of wide culture, he was in a position to indulge his enthusiasm for the arts to the full. At the same time he acquired a fine town mansion in the newly developed Kensington Palace Gardens and an estate in Scotland.

It was not, therefore, surprising that in 1851 he should have been nominated one of the Commissioners for the Great Exhibition. So enthusiastically did he address himself to his task that he was rewarded not only with a baronetcy but also with the close friendship of the Prince Consort.

In this charming watercolour by Mulready he is shown in the company of his wife, a most talented pianist who later became a close friend of Liszt, his elder daughter, Laura, who never married but who, under the name of Roderick Gunwale, was to achieve such fame as the author of a series of three-volume novels of naval life as to earn for herself the title of the 'Queen of Mudie's', and, on his knee, his younger daughter, the future Countess of Littlehampton.

SIR EBENEZER HORSEFERRY, Bt AND FAMILY
William Mulready, RA

The eldest daughter of the 6th Earl was very much her mother's child; of her father's enthusiasm for the outdoor life and the animal creation she showed no trace, but the artistic tastes, so long cultivated in the maternal line, she inherited to the full. The 6th Countess was on terms of delighted intimacy with many members of the Pre-Raphaelite circle and her beloved child was painted not only by Rossetti, who described her as 'a regular stunner', but also by Burne-Jones, Walter Crane, G. F. Watts (twice) and Sir Frank Dicksee. It was, however, a passion for music which dominated her early years; at that time the work of the Elizabethan composers was little known and it was to her researches that much of its later popularity was largely due. A founder-member of the Madrigal Society, her collection of sackbuts (now in the Metropolitan Museum in New York) was unique.

Curiously enough it was indirectly due to her musical interests that, in middle life, she played that prominent role in public affairs for which she is chiefly remembered. Thanks to her close friendship with Dame Ethel Smythe she embraced, shortly after the turn of the century, the cause of Women's Suffrage with all the passionate enthusiasm of her nature. Of her many well-publicised efforts in support of the cause, the most noteworthy was her gallant action in chaining herself to the railings of White's Club, albeit there were those who said that the avowed motive of the demonstration – to secure the release from Wormwood Scrubs of Mrs Pankhurst – perhaps took second place to a keen desire to embarrass her brother, a prominent member of the Committee. At the same time the deeply mystical strain in her character was satisfied by her friendship with Mrs Besant and membership of the Theosophical Society.

On the outbreak of the First World War her support for the Allied cause was whole-hearted, in marked contrast to her attitude in the previous conflict when she had been vociferously pro-Boer, and she was tireless in organising concerts of 17th-century music for the troops. After the war she paid a long visit to India and came back a practising Buddhist and a skilled performer on the sitar. She never married and died very suddenly in 1924, overwhelmed by emotion, in the front row of the stalls at a matineé performance of *The Immortal Hour*.

'FLORA'
D. G. Rossetti

Cosmo, the second child and eldest son of the 6th Earl, was educated at Eton and Christ Church, Oxford. As a young man he sat for several years as Liberal Member for Drayneflete, but he always had reservations about his leader and was unalterably opposed to Home Rule so that his translation to the Lords on the death of his father was for him a welcome release. Thereafter, when in London, he passed rather more time at Marlborough House than at Westminster. While inheriting his father's sporting tastes to the full, Newmarket rather than Lochwhistle was always his Mecca, but unfortunately despite the large number of horses he had in training, the more glittering prizes of the Turf invariably escaped him. Of his mother's artistic tastes he showed few signs, although he is known to have had a fondness for the music of Meyerbeer and was reported once to have expressed an admiration for the paintings of Rosa Bonheur. He had, while at Oxford, gained the reputation of being one of the best whist-players in the University but unfortunately he was never able in later life fully to master the intricacies of baccarat. This strange disability, combined with his persistent ill-luck on the race-course, so seriously embarrassed his finances that by the early 1890s matrimony seemed likely to provide the only solution. Normally irresolute, in a crisis the Earl always reacted swiftly and without hesitation and on the 1st of June 1892 he was joined in holy wedlock, in the sight of the most fashionable congregation which even St George's, Hanover Square, had ever known, to Miss Miriam Truffelheim of Frankfurt, only child of that well-known financier and international sportsman, Baron Truffelheim (later Sir Sigismund Truffelheim, KCVO). The Prince of Wales was best man and the honeymoon was spent at Biarritz.

'A SEASIDE SWELL'
Carlo Pellegrini

Few episodes in the Second Matabele Campaign excited such popular enthusiasm as the charge of the 27th Light Dragoons at Bhanwhana, led by Captain (as he then was) Frederick Courantsdair, second son of the 6th Earl of Littlehampton. This historic engagement, from which the Captain, thanks largely to his splendid mount, alone escaped unscathed, was duly immortalized in a noble canvas by Lady Butler (12 ft by $7\frac{1}{2}$ ft), that once hung in the billiard-room at Drayneflete but which has for some years been on loan to the Cavalry Club.* The Captain's subsequent career proved fully worthy of its auspicious opening. In the Boer War he served with distinction on the staff of General Buller, was Second-in-Command of the rear column at the Relief of Mafeking and ended the campaign as a full Colonel. In August 1914, on learning of the German ultimatum, he immediately abandoned the mutiny he was helping to organise at the Curragh and reported at once to his old friend Sir Henry Wilson and was duly appointed Second-in-Command of the 3rd Cavalry Division, taking over the command early in 1915. Throughout the following terrible years he never once lost his faith in ultimate victory and always managed in the face of appalling difficulties to keep his beloved cavlary in tip-top shape waiting for the final breakthrough. When at last this came, so impetuous was his advance through the enemy lines that, as one of his close companions-in-arms remarked at the time, 'it was dam' lucky for Freddy that the referee blew his whistle when he did.'

After the war he served in India, Egypt and as GOC Northern Command, retiring with rank of full General in 1933.

On the outbreak of the last war, he at once offered his services to the War Office, but after a short spell in the military censorship retired to devote himself full time to the organisation and command of the Drayneflete Home Guard. In this role his most notable exploit was the disposal of a large unexploded bomb which fell in the middle of the Common which he insisted, brushing aside his Sergeant-Major's protests, in defusing himself. The enormous crater which resulted was subsequently laid out as a Memorial Bog Garden, at the expense of the present Earl who presented it to the town at a simple service of dedication, conducted by Canon Fontwater, on the fifth anniversary of his uncle's death.

* Where it is likely to remain. R.S.

'THE LAST CHARGE OF THE 27TH' [*a detail*]
Lady Butler

The second and favourite daughter of the 6th Earl shared all her male parent's tastes to the full. As soon as she was out of the nursery her days were spent either in the stables or in the kennels. Although an accomplished and vigorous performer in eightsome reels, of her mother's deep love of music she showed no further sign, and her appreciation of the fine arts was strictly limited to the works of Sartorius and Sir Francis Grant. A superb horsewoman, her exploits, not only with the Drayneflete, but also with the Quorn, the Pytchley and the Galway Blazers, were legendary. In 1893 she married Colonel Sir Jasper Wickham-Stench, Bt, sometime joint Master of the Bicester. The marriage, although unblessed with offspring, was a complete success, but unfortunately the Colonel, who was some years her senior, and whose health had been weakened by prolonged service on the North-West Frontier, predeceased her by many years. 'I am rather afraid', she used frequently to remark, 'that poor dear Jasper was not quite up to my weight.'

The accompanying portrait was presented to her by followers of the Drayneflete at a moving ceremony at the New Year's Meet in 1935 when she celebrated the fiftieth anniversary of her first appearance with the pack and her twenty-fifth as Master. During the last war, when most of her own, and as much as she could lay hands on of her household's, rations went straight to the kennels, she not only managed to hunt twice a week but, with a view to saving petrol, also organised and commanded a mounted squadron of the WVS which did sterling work, delivering 'meals on wheels' at a far greater speed and over a much larger area than would have been possible on foot. Her end was blissful; she died, if not in harness, at least in the harness-room, where she collapsed into the arms of the whipper-in after consuming a friendly glass of cherry brandy to celebrate the new litter to which her favourite bitch had just given birth. She was in her eighty-second year and her last words, very strongly spoken, were 'Gone away!'

THE LADY AGATHA WICKHAM-STENCH
Sir Alfred Munnings, PRA

The youngest of the three sons of the 6th Earl was, when young, handicapped by ill-health. After a very short period at Eton he had to be removed to warmer climes and was educated privately until he went up to Brasenose College, Oxford, where he came under the influence of Mr Walter Pater. After two formative years he came down without taking a degree, and was thenceforth to be found at the centre of that artistic circle presided over by his mother, or at the Café Royal. An occasional contributor to *The Yellow Book*, he also published a beautifully produced volume of translation of Pierre Louÿs and a slim volume of poems, some of which were set to music by his friend Reynaldo Hahn.

In the spring of 1895 he left, rather suddenly, for abroad and from then on resided permanently at the charming villa inherited from his mother above Fiesole which his exquisite hospitality and informed taste rendered a place of pilgrimage for three generations of art-lovers. In the Florentine social life of the day he played a notable role, enjoying the friendship of Vernon Lee, Lucie Duff Gordon, Ouida, Bernard Berenson and Mrs Keppel, although, curiously enough, never being on speaking terms with more than two of them at any one time.

On the outbreak of the last war he was forced to abandon his beloved Florence and take refuge with his niece-by-marriage, the present Countess, who kindly gave him shelter at Drayneflete. Here, despite the close proximity of his brother Frederick and a company of ATS stationed in the Abbey, both of which he found uncongenial, he settled down quite happily, occupying his leisure with the production of an exquisite *petit-point* carpet (now in the Green Drawing-Room) which he laughingly referred to as 'my war-work'.

On the cessation of hostilities he returned at once to the Villa Dolce which he found neglected but mercifully undamaged, and where ten years later he died in his sleep. To his niece, for whom he had developed a warm affection, he left his portrait by Boldini and his celebrated collection of Fabergé Easter eggs. The remainder of his estate passed to his faithful valet Alfredo.

THE HON ALGERNON COURANTSDAIR
Boldini

In the Royal Academy Exhibition of 1881 the Picture of the Year was unquestionably *Pussy's Going Bye-Byes* by the President himself; universally acclaimed, even Mr Ruskin could not withold his admiration, which in the circumstances was magnanimous, declaring it to be the equal of the finest work of Kate Greenaway and Fra Angelico.

The original of this charming study of childhood was the Lady Ethel, youngest child of the 6th Earl of Littlehampton, who had inherited to the full her father's love of all forms of animal life. Generally acknowledged to be the most beautiful débutante of 1897 it was confidently expected that she would make a brilliant match. Alas, it was not to be! A highly romantic nature and High Church leanings led her to reject all her numerous suitors and to fall hopelessly in love with a penniless curate at All Saints, Margaret Street. Her brother, a staunch Evangelical, was at first firmly opposed to any idea of marriage but even when, under his mother's influence, he had been induced to give his grudging consent, the course of true love did not run smooth. During a protracted engagement the bridegroom-to-be struggled manfully with his conscience and his vicar, who held strong views on clerical celibacy; but shortly before coming to a final decision, never robust and exhausted by this inner conflict, he succumbed to the influenza epidemic then raging.

For the Lady Ethel the blow was severe and for a time she contemplated entering an Anglican sisterhood. Finally dissuaded by her family from so drastic a step, she thenceforth devoted her life to good works. Naturally it was animal welfare which excited her keenest enthusiasm – lost dogs and stray cats never had so doughty a champion, and many a Littlehampton water-trough still testifies to her solicitude for cart-horses – but her compassion knew no limits and was freely extended to Distressed Gentlefolk, Sons of the Clergy and Fallen Women. No woman of her generation organized more tombolas or opened more bazaars, and in 1911 she was appointed Lady-in-Waiting to HRH Princess Marie Louise.

Today, well on in her tenth decade, she still presides over innumerable committees in her house in Cadogan Square, which she refused to leave even during the height of the Blitz, surrounded by four Pekinese, six Siamese cats, a score of budgerigars and a parrot.

'PUSSY'S GOING BYE-BYES'
Sir John Everett Millais, Bt, PRA

Miss Miriam Truffelheim was the only daughter of Baron Truffelheim, the financial genius who reorganised the KuK Eisenbahn
Gesellschaft, established the Bosnia-Herzegovina Handelsbank
and was ennobled by the Emperor Franz Josef. An intimate friend
of HRH the Prince of Wales, as was his daughter, the Baron,
having previously adopted British nationality, was created KCVO
in the Coronation Honours Lists. At the same time he acquired
substantial interests in Johannesburg. His daughter, whose wit
and beauty had created something of a sensation when she was
launched on London Society at a great ball in her father's
residence in Park Lane, soon took her place alongside Daisy,
Princess of Pless, Lady Warwick and Mrs Cornwallis-West as one
of the toasts of the town without whom no smart house-party
could be considered a success.

Once established in the old Littlehampton House in St James's
Square, the new Countess promptly embarked on a social career
of dazzling brilliance; balls, routs and supper-parties followed
each other in quick succession and during the shooting season the
Abbey was the scene of many a high-spirited gathering. Possessed
of a robust sense of humour and a gift for mimicry, she was the
organiser of innumerable practical jokes, of which, perhaps, the
most celebrated was the occasion when she donned a false
moustache and a monocle and won the egg-and-spoon race at the
Vicarage Fête in the character of Monsieur de Soveral. Another
time, disguised as an old gipsy-woman, she went round an Ascot
house-party reading palms; unfortunately in reading Mrs Keppel's she proved a little too accurate and for a time her relations
with her sovereign were characterized by an unusual coolness.

When, after the birth of her only daughter, it became clear that
all hope of an heir must be abandoned; the Earl and Countess
gradually drifted apart and it was no surprise when in 1905 they
separated by mutual agreement. Thenceforward the Countess
spent much of her time in her beautiful villa on Cap Ferrat,
marrying first Prince Annibale Brutafigura (marriage dissolved
1921) and then Hiram van Stickleback III, the well-known
international yachtsman, on whose Long Island estate she died in
1943.

MIRIAM, COUNTESS OF LITTLEHAMPTON
J. S. Sargent, RA

The break-up of his first marriage in 1905 was a source of considerable distress to the 7th Earl and in the late summer of that year he went for a couple of weeks, before the grouse season opened, to take the restorative waters of Harrogate. While there he made the acquaintance of a Miss Lottie Dolores (*née* Bloggs) of Tulse Hill who was appearing in the No 2 touring company of *San Toy*. Acquaintance ripened into friendship, friendship into love, and in the following spring they were joined in wedlock.

The bride was the daughter of one of the most respected publicans in South London and her mother had, in her youth, gained a modest but deserved fame by being shot from a cannon twice nightly at the Westminster Aquarium. Many of the Earl's acquaintances were sceptical about the future happiness of a pair with such widely differing backgrounds, but they were soon rebuked. The new Countess, who had inherited much of her father's business sense, at once set about bringing order into the 7th Earl's rather confused finances, and she handled his dependants and the domestic staff on his various estates with the same firmness that had gained her the ungrudging respect of the patrons of the Saloon Bar at the Plumbers' Arms where she had, from time to time, been accustomed to help out while 'resting'.

Early in 1906 she gave birth to a daughter and in the following year the longed-for heir. Outside her family her main interests were the Conservative Party and charity; the former made Little-hampton House, in St James's Square, one of the principal rallying-points of the stern, unbending Tories during the constitutional crisis of 1911, the latter gained her the close friendship of her sister-in-law the Lady Ethel who, when it came to arranging charity matinées, found her experience invaluable. Only once, however, did she herself ever again perform in public, and then involuntarily; at a great Victory Bonds rally at the Albert Hall in 1916 she stepped into the gap left by Dame Clara Butt (who had had the misfortune to be knocked down by a Boy Scout on a bicycle during a Zeppelin raid the night before) and led a wildly enthusiastic audience in the singing of 'Keep the Home Fires Burning'.

She survived her husband by many years, dying early in 1952, universally mourned; at her memorial service at St Paul's Knightsbridge it was standing room only.

FAMILY PHOTOGRAPH ALBUM

'OURSELVES AND TUM-TUM' – DRAYNEFLETE, CHRISTMAS
1904

CECIL BEATOV

CHARLOTTE, COUNTESS OF LITTLEHAMPTON
ON HER MARRIAGE AT THE CORONATION
OF HM KING GEORGE VI

The 7th Earl's only daughter by his first marriage was christened Mabel, a name which she intensely disliked and for which, when she came out shortly after the First World War, she substituted Amethyst. In the London of the roaring 'twenties few roared louder than she; a ring-leader of the Bright Young People, no party was complete without her and her own entertainments, often given, much to the annoyance of her stepmother, in Little-hampton House, invariably made the headlines. Of these the most celebrated, indeed notorious, was the Bible Ball where all the guests came as characters from Holy Writ with the hostess, predictably, as Salome. Unfortunately the evening ended disastrously when 'Tago' Staplehurst, who had come as St Paul, fell out of the basket in which he was being lowered from a third-storey window and broke his neck. Shortly after this she abandoned London for a while, to the unconcealed delight of the Countess, for an apartment in the Rue du Bac, where she soon gathered round her a band of artistic and distinguished friends. She smoked opium with Cocteau, played duets with Poulenc and was dressed by Coco Chanel, gaining for herself the affectionate nickname of 'La Vache sur le Toit'.

However, despite her Parisian success, she did not neglect her old friends and commuted to London regularly during the Season, and it was there that she first encountered Evelyn Waugh who has left a vivid account of the meeting in his recently published diaries: 'After dinner went on to party of *****. Everyone beastly drunk. Bruno Hat and some filthy dago sodomizing on the sofa. Found myself next to a Lesbian friend of Hamish, whom I at once suspected of being a flagellant, who bored me to death talking about people in Paris I didn't know. However, when Hamish told me she was Willy Drayneflete's half-sister, decided to accept her offer of a lift home. Discovered in the cab that she was not a Lesbian but *was* a whipper. Woke up sore and exhausted and had to go straight round to White's for a couple of brandies-and-crême-de-menthes.'

The year following this entry, she was married in Paris to a well-known interior decorator, the Marquis de Pernod-Framboise.

The Marquise predeceased her husband by several years, dying in 1940 as a result of a rather mysterious car smash after a late-night party in Nairobi.

LADY A à LONGCHAMPS
Van Dongen

Ursula, the elder child of the 7th Earl's second marriage, inherited her paternal grandmother's artistic enthusiasm in full measure. This, together with the markedly unconventional streak which she displayed when still a child, while giving no satisfaction to her mother, at once endeared her to her Aunt Flora, who not only encouraged her artistic ambitions but paid for her to study at the Slade. Social life she scorned and only attended débutante dances under maternal pressure and the sole country-house she could be induced to visit was, occasionally, Garsington. All the Countess's efforts to encourage her daughter to conform to a way of life suitable to her rank were finally thwarted on the death of the Lady Flora who left her niece the whole of her fortune, thus enabling her to set herself up in a large studio in Fitzroy Square. Like her benefactress, she developed, as time went on, a keen interest in social questions and during the 1930s she marched in countless processions to abolish the Means Test, she denounced Fascist aggression in Abyssinia from innumerable platforms, and finally took off to drive an ambulance in beleaguered Madrid.

At the outbreak of war she returned to her easel but with the invasion of Russia she immediately identified herself with the Allied cause. She organised exhibitions of Soviet handicrafts, sat on committees and often, after a heavy day's work, would spend the night-hours writing 'Open a Second Front Now' on the walls of the Middlesex Hospital. After the final victory the joy she naturally experienced at the coming to power of a Labour government was soon eroded, and she was back on the barricades. It was during an Aldermaston march that she first met her husband, Dr Wraclaw Golobeck, a Croatian economist, at that time a lecturer at LSE, subsequently a fellow of Balliol College, Oxford. Their marriage has always been a completely unselfish relationship, both taking an active part in the struggle against Imperialism, Neo-Colonialism and Male Chauvinism. Organising Secretary of Peeresses for Peace, President of the Boar's Hill Branch of the International Maoist Association and an active patroness of Women's Lib, she still finds time for literature, and last year her book *The Life and Thought of John Berger* was awarded the coveted Prix Femina-Vie Malheureuse.

'URSULA'
Mark Gertler

William succeeded his father as 8th Earl in 1937. A sunny-natured lad he was educated at Eton and Christ Church, Oxford, where he took a leading part in all the social activities of the day. Naturally a nervous speaker, the need he experienced to fortify himself before his few appearances at the Union frequently obscured the depth and originality of his political thinking, but at Bullingdon dinners he invariably proved an unqualified success. Over the sticks he displayed a skill to rival that of Lord Longford (Frank Pakenham as he then was) while his performance as Sir Andrew Aguecheek in *Twelfth Night* gained for him a reputation that extended far beyond the OUDS. On going down, after his final and, alas, unsuccessful attempt to pass 'Divvers', he entered the Household Cavalry and in 1931, after several successful seasons as the principal 'deb's delight' of his day, he married. Shortly afterwards, on the occasion of his father's ninth stroke, he resigned his commission in order to give more time to helping his mother in the management of the Estate. On the outbreak of war he rejoined his regiment and served with distinction in North Africa and Italy. Early in 1945 he was 'dropped' on the headquarters of the Rumanian Resistance which existed, he was pained to discover, almost exclusively in the imagination of GHQ Cairo. However, he was able, after many difficulties, to make his way to Turkey disguised as Princess Bibesco.

His Lordship's appearances in the Upper House, although infrequent, have not been ineffective and it was largely due to his efforts that the Second Reading of the Hedgehogs Protection Bill was successfully carried. Although shunning the limelight, his influence, particularly in local affairs, is great and in 1970 his tact and discretion were largely responsible for the re-routing of the M17 through a neighbour's park some fifteen miles distant from the Abbey.

AS A CHILD
Jacques Emile Blanche

WHEN
VISCOUNT DRAYNEFLETE
Sir Oswald Birley, RA

Lady Littlehampton is the only daughter of Sir Julian Manifest, Bt and the Lady Claribel Manifest, third daughter of the 5th Marquess of Pontefract. Her father, who came of a long line of distinguished diplomatists, was himself the grandson of Sir Tresham Manifest and the 3rd Countess of Littlehampton and, as various portraits in the present collection so clearly show, it was from her celebrated great-grandmother that his daughter inherited her looks. Her youth was passed almost entirely in London and the English countryside as her father served his whole career in the Foreign Office and was never known to have crossed the Channel except for a single weekend at Dieppe.

Coming out at the end of the 1920s her vivacity and beauty rendered her outstanding even in a generation which included such glamorous contemporaries as Miss Nancy Mitford, Miss Maureen Guinness and Miss Rosemary Hope-Vere. After her wedding to her distant cousin, Viscount Drayneflete, which packed St Margaret's and took up six pages of *The Tatler*, the young couple settled down in a small but beautifully decorated house in Hill Street which served as the background for many a gay party, duly chronicled by Lord Donegal and Patrick Balfour.

With the outbreak of war the new Countess (her husband had succeeded to the title on the death of his father in 1937) at once revealed her true character, which had hitherto lain largely undetected behind what seemed, perhaps a rather frivolous façade. At various times she worked in MI5, MI6, SOE, PWE and the YWCA as well as constantly liaising with the Free French. In 1945 she was attached to our Embassy in Cairo, where her lovely flat on Gezireh quickly became a home from a home for all members of White's serving in that theatre.

Since the war she has frequently thought of standing for Parliament but as on some matters she is far to the right of Mr Enoch Powell, and on others well to the left of Mr Michael Foot, she has never yet succeeded in being adopted by any of the three major parties. However, she has done sterling work as Chairman of the Planning Committee of her local council, where she sits as an Independent, and it is largely due to her efforts that the Drayneflete Green Belt is still intact.

AT THE TIME OF
HER COMING OUT
Sir John Lavery, RA

WHEN FULLY OUT
Augustus John, OM, RA

Few débutantes of the 1950s aroused such general admiration or received so much publicity as the 8th Earl's elder daughter. Lively, energetic and scornful of convention – she was put on probation for the first time for 'pushing' cannabis at Queen Charlotte's Ball – she soon became a leading member of the so-called 'Chelsea Set'. At various times she ran a disco, a bistro and a boutique, but finally wearying of the shoddy glitter of the King's Road, after a short spell at the University of Sussex, she took up social work and moved to Peckham Rye. Here she produced her celebrated best-seller *Up the Spout*, a fearless and exhaustive study of the manners and morals of darkest Lewisham which went into three (rather small) editions and gained for her the Vanessa Redgrave Memorial Award.

In 1963 she announced her engagement to Sid Krackle, the well-known dramatist and pillar of The Royal Court, but broke it off after the birth of their first child.

Some years later she founded The Theatre of the Totally Absurd in a converted gasometer on Hackney Marshes which opened, and closed, with the celebrated production of *Where the Rainbow Ends* in the nude, with very incidental music by Stockhausen and the dialogue rewritten in very basic English. Then, in 1971, after a short period as Fashion Editor of *Private Eye* and a brief appearance in the chorus-line of *Hair* she retired to Majorca, where she is at the moment engaged on writing her autobiography.

Despite the fullness of her life and the wide range of her interests she has always remained an affectionate and dutiful daughter, and, although she is still unmarried, a devoted mother.

'JENNIFER'
John Bratby

Torquil, the son and heir of the present Earl, had a perfectly conventional upbringing – Eton, which he left under the usual cloud, and King's College, Cambridge, whence he was sent down in his second year for organizing a pro-Lumumba demonstration during the Annual Carol Service. Coming to London he naturally gravitated to his sister's set in the King's Road where, having always been handy with a Kodak, he set himself up as a freelance photographer. Unfortunately, being only a Viscount, and with a courtesy title at that, he soon found the competition of the Earls too great and abandoned photography for music. As he had always had a charming voice – his rendering of 'O for the Wings of a Dove' had aroused unavowable emotions in many an Etonian breast at numerous school concerts – and had also inherited much of his paternal grandmother's histrionic ability, he soon made a name for himself as a vocalist with several of the pop groups flourishing at that period. In 1969 he formed his own ensemble, the Draynes, and was soon figuring regularly in the charts. In the following year he hit the jack-pot with his highly personal version of 'Jesus Wants Me for a Sunbeam', which remained Top of the Pops for no less than thirteen weeks in succession. After an immensely successful tour of the United States he concluded a very gratifying contract with ITV and now enjoys a Saturday-night 'spot' on no fewer than five stations. He has recently acquired a large mansion with two swimming-pools at St George's Hill, Weybridge, a yacht and a villa in Barbados. He married, in 1972, Anna Maria Teresa Tombola (Miss British Honduras 1971) and they have one son, the Master of Lochwhistle. When interviewed on television about her son's achievement, Lady Littlehampton expressed great pride in his success, stressing that he was completely self-taught; his father said that he, personally, did not think he was a patch on Nellie Wallace.

VISCOUNT DRAYNEFLETE
From the sleeve of his current LP

Unlike her elder sister, the second daughter of the present Earl has always shunned the social limelight. Inheriting to the full her Great-Aunt Agatha's equestrian enthusiasm, she remained until her marriage firmly based on Drayneflete, devoting herself to pony clubs and hunter trials. Great, therefore, was the general surprise, in which it is suggested she herself shared, when her engagement was announced to a young man who was nursing the constituency as a Conservative, whom she had met quite casually at a local point-to-point.

Basil Cantilever is the only son of that distinguished architect, Sir Frederick Cantilever, OM, RA, PRIBA, who has made so many changes in London's skyline during the last quarter of a century. On coming down from Cambridge he entered his father's office where he was quick to concentrate on the organizational rather than the creative side of his profession. In 1963, he joined the board of Cantilever Securities which he built up into one of the largest of property companies and of which in 1967 he became Chairman. At the same time he did sterling work in local government, becoming a member both of the Westminster City Council and the GLC. Two years later he was returned for Drayneflete at a by-election and at the same time had the satisfaction of learning that his family firm had won the international competition for the design of a Parliamentary Sports Club and Bingo Hall which it is hoped will shortly be erected on the site of Inigo Jones's Banqueting House. A year previously he had succeeded to his father's seat on the Royal Fine Art Commission. His reputation in the House stands high and at the last Government reshuffle he was appointed PPS to the Minister of Exploitation.

In his wife's family, however, it must regretfully be admitted that admiration is tempered with criticism. The present Earl's prejudice against all politicians, particularly in the Lower House, has not diminished with the years, while Lady Littlehampton's deepest feelings were outraged by the demolition of St Ursula-inside-the-Wardrobe (with which the family had had such a long connection) acquired by her son-in-law from the Church Commissioners in 1968 for a very reasonable sum, and the erection, on the site, of Cantilever House, a thirty-storey block of offices all of which still happily remain unlet.

BASIL CANTILEVER ESQ AND THE LADY PATRICIA CANTILEVER
David Hockney

Thelwell